Millionaire Success Secrets

Jason A. Scott

Copyright © 2021 Jason A. Scott
All rights reserved.

Table of Contents

Chapter 1: Introduction 1
Chapter 2: Morning Ritual 3
Chapter 3: Affirmation 11
Chapter 4: Visualization 14
Chapter 5: Positive Reminder 16
Chapter 6: Principle of 80/20 19
Chapter 7: Principle of 99/1 22
Chapter 8: Learn from History 24
Chapter 9: Travel 26
Chapter 10: Little things matter & Daily Magic Moment 31
Chapter 11: Daily Wisdom on Life, Time & Money 34
Chapter 12: Meditation & Making Choices 38
Chapter 13: How the World Operates 42
Chapter 14: Positive Attitude and Happiness 47
Chapter 15: Self Discipline & Perspectives 51
Chapter 16: Rules of Life 53
Chapter 17: Gratitude & Motivation 58
Chapter 18: Positive Mental Toughness 61
Chapter 19: Power of "Invisible Mentors" & Acting the Part 63
Chapter 20: Goal Setting & Communication 65
Chapter 21: Dealing with Adversity 69
Chapter 22: Proper Frame of Mind 74
Chapter 23: Habits 77
Chapter 24: Family 79

Chapter 25: Business 81
Chapter 26: Personal Finance & Attitude Towards Money 88
Chapter 27: Obsession to Detail & Watching Expenses 93
Chapter 28: Health & Zen Moments 98
Chapter 29: Relationship with Others 104
Chapter 30: Dating 113
Chapter 31: Managing People 116
Chapter 32: Communication & The Art of Selling 120
Chapter 33: Investing 123
Chapter 34: Commercial Real Estate 128
Chapter 35: Goal Setting & Visualization 131
Chapter 36: Negotiation 133
Chapter 37: Art of Asking for More 136
Chapter 38: Living with Purpose 139
Chapter 39: Money & Simple Living 141
Chapter 40: Retirement & Charity 146
Chapter 41: Becoming a Monetized YouTuber in 3 weeks 149
Chapter 42: Conclusion 156
Chapter 43: Book Recommendations 157

Chapter 1: Introduction

Before going over all the life hacks I have learned throughout the years, I want to tell you a little about my background. I have accomplished quite a bit in my 47 years! Of course, this doesn't qualify me to tell you what to do or not to do with your life. Still, by sharing my experiences, perhaps I can help you achieve success with your life, whether personally, financially, physically, or mentally.

I talked a lot about my background in my first book, "Millionaire Landlord Secrets," so I will only go over the basics here. I graduated from the University of California when I was 23. Over the following 12 years, I held eight different jobs and was fired from all of them! After some soul searching, I finally realized that maybe I was just not good at working for someone else. I then started my own business in the medical field when I turned 35. After saving up some side money, I decided to invest in commercial real estate, and the rest is history. Ten years later, at 45 years old, I now have a net worth in the eight figures. But that is not the best part! Approximately 80% of my net worth consists of assets that are generating passive income for me at this very moment. I tell you this not to impress you, but to impress upon you that my system works. It works for me, and it can work for you too!

Over the years, I have created several systems customized to my business that streamline operations and generate income without requiring too much of my time. I have also come up with many life hacks that have simplified my lifestyle, resulting in me being constantly happy! I genuinely believe that my success has a lot to do with all the life hacks and principles that I follow and have practiced over the years. I would like to share them with as many people as possible! Luck always plays a part in any success story, but my hard work and the principles I follow are the main drivers behind my success at achieving financial freedom at such a young age. People sometimes ask me why I want to share my secrets with the world. As a teacher and life coach, the answer is simple: it will make me happy if just a single person uses my life hacks and becomes successful. Seeing others succeed with my help gives me a double dose of happiness and fulfillment.

I have learned many hard lessons along the path to success that I wish someone would have warned me about ahead of time! I could have saved so much time, money, and heartache. At the same time, I also realize that there are many things best learned by oneself, just like a newborn learning to walk. They have to fall many times before taking those first steps, and before long, they're running on their own! It's the same in life. Most of the life hacks you will read about in this book, I learned through trial and error, and I have paid my tuition with money and time. In this book, I will share with you what I have learned and what principles (or life hacks) I created for my life to live efficiently and productively.

The life hacks in this book are arranged into chapters based on when it is the best time or place to use these principles. All the chapters are listed in the Table of Contents at the beginning of the book. There is no "best" order; you are welcome to jump to whichever chapter most catches your interest. However, I do recommend that you read the entire book, as I believe you will greatly benefit from all the principles.

Chapter 2: Morning Ritual

Since I was a young boy, I wanted to become an affluent person with a comfortable lifestyle. I wanted to study all the famous millionaires and billionaires to see what they did to become successful. So I read tons of autobiographies and articles about famous rich people, and I jotted down detailed notes on how they thought and what they did. Then I wrote down the top 10 things wealthy people do when they first wake up in the morning. Surprisingly, the top 3 things on the list were always the same! They are exercise, reading, and meditation, in that particular sequence. I figured that if I wanted to be wealthy, I needed to do what wealthy people did. That was my "a-ha" moment! Ever since that moment, I have woken up at 5 am and completed those three things before checking my phone or doing anything else. Because I consider my morning ritual to be one of the essential requirements for becoming successful, I will spend a significant amount of time discussing it in this book. I genuinely believe that having a great morning will set you up for a great rest of your day. Each time I do my entire morning ritual, I have an efficient and productive day; it is an essential part of success.

Good morning rituals all start the night before when I visualize myself happily waking up to do cardio. I say to myself, "Yes, I am going to work out in 6 hours! I am going to be better than 99% of other people since they are all still sleeping while I'm getting happier and healthier."

Imagine that it is 5 am, and your alarm wakes you. The first 5 seconds of waking up are the hardest, so don't think - just get up and make the bed! Then do your three thank-you's (we'll talk about exactly what these are later) and immediately start your workout. Avoid the temptation to look at your phone by leaving it in another room the night before. Congratulations, you just won your first battle of the day! You get to win it every morning!

I made an acronym for my morning routines: CRM, which stands for Cardio, Reading, and Meditation. I start each day by exercising on my elliptical or treadmill at 5 am for 45 minutes, then read for about 30 minutes, and finally meditate for 15 minutes. The entire CRM should be complete by 6:30 am. Imagine that by 6:30 am, while most people are still sleeping, you have already finished the most vital things you need to do in the day! Not only did you get a big head start, but you are already ahead of 99% of the people in this world! If you do this and nothing else for the rest of the day, you have still done well since what you do in the morning sets you up for how the rest of the day will go. Let's go into more detail about how the CRM process works.

Start your day with CRM: Cardio, Reading, and Meditation.

The first step is the C. Every morning, as soon as I jump out of bed, I say out loud three things I am grateful for. These can be things, people, or events. For example, this morning, when I woke up, I said, "Thank you, world, for letting me wake up this morning. Thank you, world, for this great sunny weather and the amazing day that awaits. And thank you, grandma, for watching me from above. Thank you, thank you, thank you!" You can thank anything and anyone. Saying these thank you's out loud puts you in what I call the *Gratitude Mindset* so that you start the day with gratitude and appreciation for the past, present, future, and everything around you. I will explain this in more detail in a later chapter. For now, just remember to think of three things you're grateful for as soon as you open your eyes in the morning. Also, if you like, you can find something to thank for the rest of the day, even something small or simple. For example, I sometimes thank the roses in my backyard for the beautiful scenery and the wonderful smell they give me when I read on a nearby bench.

Millionaire Success Secrets

Start the day with gratitude and appreciation for the past, present, future, and everything around you.

The other thing I do while saying my thanks is make my bed. I refer to this as the first baby step of the day. Some people might question why this is so important. First, making your bed is very easy to do; it might only take you 5 to 10 seconds from start to finish. But the fact that you can do it consistently every morning makes it your first regular accomplishment of the day. It is the right start, and you will immediately feel a sense of getting something done right. The momentum will start building from there. So please don't make the mistake of thinking that making your bed is trivial; instead, it is the right first step! In addition, as much as you don't want to make your bed but are doing it anyway, it helps you create a good habit and builds your self-discipline. So you are killing two birds with one stone.

Now we come to the second part of CRM: R is for Reading. I have read over 120 books in the past five years, which might seem like a lot, but it is only about one book every two weeks. The only thing I regret is not reading more books sooner. I've heard that Bill Gates and Warren Buffet read at least one book per day, so I am way behind! I'm not comparing myself to the two wealthiest people on earth; I simply think of them as my *invisible mentors,* and I want to imitate everything they do. I don't know of any wealthy person who does not enjoy reading. So if your goal is to be successful, read!

Read books written by people who have accomplished great things in their lives, study them, and then do the same things they do. I think of such people as my invisible mentors who are always there to cheer me on and pick me up on my path to success. As long as I have the same mentality and mindset as my mentors, I can accomplish any goal I set my mind to. After that, the sky is the limit! The nice thing about this approach is that you can have as many mentors as you like and learn from all of them just by reading their books. Think about that. All the most successful people in the world are sharing their knowledge with you. There is simply nothing else better when it comes to learning successful tips.

Jason A. Scott

If your goal is to be successful, read!

When you read a book, how do you get the most out of it? I usually read using my amazon kindle e-reader, and I read about 10% of any given book per day. Depending on how long the book is, this can take about 20-40 minutes every morning. When I start reading a book for the first time, I highlight any particularly important sections. Kindle will let you type in notes, so I rephrase those key points in my own words and organize them as notes. Once I finish reading the book, I immediately go back and reread all my highlights and notes. In the meantime, I think about how to apply what I've learned from the book to my business or lifestyle. So many people go through books and promptly forget all they learned as soon as they finish reading. What a complete waste of time! Instead, read with a purpose. Learn something from every book that will help you become a better person, run your business more efficiently, or improve your overall well-being. I might read a 500-page book that takes me weeks to finish, but I am satisfied and happy even if I learn just one thing from it. Knowledge is so rare and precious, so be thankful whenever you can learn something new that you can use to better yourself.

What kind of books should you read? Personally, I read with a purpose, so I look for books that will either help me grow my business or improve my well-being. Business books have subjects such as communicating with employees more effectively, providing better customer service, negotiating, investing, operating a rental property more efficiently, and tips on how to prioritize my time. Books that help me personally have subjects such as traveling, piloting, tennis, how to think and speak better, how to deal with challenges, how to focus, how to talk to myself, how to deal with difficult people or situations, how to be more self-disciplined, how to stay motivated, and how to have a more fulfilling and happier life.

As you can see, the first type of book helps me with my business or anything *external*, and the second type of book helps me with anything *internal*. I genuinely believe that it's necessary to have a balanced internal and external life to achieve one's ultimate well-being. If you don't know what books to start with, I provide a list of book recommendations at the end of this book for you.

I also enjoy listening to classical music, especially when I read. I think music from the Baroque period somehow stimulus my mind when I am learning things. Try out different kinds of music and see what works best for you.

I currently run two types of businesses: a medical office business and a commercial real estate business. When I started each business, I had zero experience and didn't know anyone in a related industry, so I had to learn everything from scratch. This is where reading books comes in handy! Before I started the commercial real estate business, I picked up 22 real estate-related books from Amazon to learn about the subject. Books taught me about acquiring properties, financing buildings, managing tenants, and reporting taxes. I read books written by authors who did what I wanted to do and succeeded. I learned as much as I could from those authors to avoid making the same mistakes they did, and was able to achieve my goals reasonably quickly after that. I consider every single one of those authors to be my invisible mentor, and I am forever grateful to them. As far as I'm concerned, I have 22 real estate experts with hundreds of years of hands-on experience in the industry between them, supporting me 24/7. How could I not succeed?

As you can see, reading books is key to becoming successful. Read as much as you possibly can! Sometimes, when I tell people to read more, I hear all kinds of reasons why they don't or can't read more; usually, they say they are too busy or don't have the time. I then ask, "So you have been busy doing such and such. Are you happy with the results?" That usually gets them to think a bit and maybe prompts them to read more. But unfortunately, most people tell me they will *try* to read more and then just give up on it in a couple of weeks and go back to their busy yet unproductive lives. Don't be those people!

Jason A. Scott

The last part of CRM is meditation. I remember that when I first started meditating, I hated it. I couldn't sit still for more than 2 minutes. I would constantly think about what I needed to do next, the people I needed to call, the things I needed to do, or why I was wasting my time sitting and doing "nothing." But after a while, I got used to meditating for at least 15 minutes per day. Now meditation might just be one of the most important parts of my day! Yes, I still have thoughts shifting in and out of my mind, but that's ok; I just let those thoughts flow in and then back out of me, and I also control the urge to get up and look at my phone. If those transient thoughts are important, I'll remember them when the meditation is over. If I can't remember them afterward, then they weren't that important after all.

There are many free meditation apps available; pick one that you like to use. Just turn on your app, take a deep breath, and follow the instructions. With the soothing music in the background, it's pretty relaxing.

When meditating, imagine that time itself has stopped, focus on your deep breathing, let thoughts come in and back out again, and just be. Say to yourself, "I am inhaling fresh, healthy air, and I am exhaling toxins, disease, and stress."

When I breathe in, I visualize that I am breathing in air, love, nutrients, and positive energy into every cell and organ in my body. I hold each breath for 5 seconds so my cells and organs can absorb all the good stuff. When I exhale, I breathe out all the toxins and negativity. In the meantime, my mind is completely blank with no thoughts at all. At this moment, my internal thoughts and external physical body are together as one, what I called the Zen Moment.

The Zen Moment occurs when I am completely relaxed and energized at the same time. I am at the top of my game, mentally and physically, to start this fantastic day ahead of me. Some readers might think this is some crazy religious cult stuff, but it is not. I am not religious by any means, and I don't believe in voodoo or some weird supernatural element; meditation simply works. Meditation is a simple way to bring peace of mind in this fast pace world. It is hard to explain, but I strongly encourage you just to give it a try, and you will benefit tremendously.

For those who are beginners to meditation and do not know where to start, I recommend an app called "Mediations" (see picture below). It gives you verbal instructions on what to think while meditating while soft music plays in the background. I find it to be very calming.

Chapter 3: Affirmation

In addition to waking up with gratitude, performing the CRM, and taking baby steps toward self-discipline and success by making your bed, I also recommend reading the affirmation below out loud to yourself before starting your day. Doing so will help you get into a healthy mindset. While I read the following list aloud, I also visualize my *ideal self* where I have a fit body, flat abs, a bulging chest, and where my whole body is full of energy, ready to explore this fantastic day. The list of affirmations is below, and the items in parentheses are the specific things that I either think or actions I take while I am saying those phrases out loud. Most importantly, I say these words with a big smile on my face, and I truly believe these words as well.

- I am happy (say it with a HUGE smile on your face).

- I am positive, smiling, and laughing.

- I am healthy (look at my young, ageless face and my super-fit body with rock hard abs)

- I am bright & filled with energy; I am successful; I think abundance.

- I am focused (because that is where my energy will flow).

- I am efficient & productive.

- I am responsible. What can I do now? (instead of complaining, I am taking action to better the situation.)

- I am calmed & relaxed. Peace of mind is the crown jewel of wisdom.

- I am always confident & prepared.

- I am thoughtful & considerate.

- I am grateful, I replace expectation with appreciation, I always have an Attitude of Gratitude. Things I am thankful for can be in the Past, Present, or the Future (Past: life I lived. Present: things I have now. Future: the time I keep on living).

- I am self-disciplined, I love myself, and many people love me.

- I choose deferred gratification over instant reward.

- I am resourceful. I am always in control of my destiny.

- I am honest to myself & others.

- I dictate my successful path & future reality.

- I slow down and enjoy the Moment.

- I live and breathe positive energy into every living moment in life. Life is good; life is easy; all good things come to me.

- I do *The One Thing* I need to do to get 80% of the results with 20% of the effort.

- I don't worry because worrying doesn't achieve anything. Instead, I take action so that I'm prepared.

- I don't stress about things out of my control; I will handle things when they happen.

- I avoid the 3Cs: Complaints, Criticisms, and Comparisons

- I turn everything into something positive by changing how I look at things. When I wait in traffic, it gives me time to relax & think. It's my own ME time.

- I expect to be treated the best to get the best. "Why not me, and why not now?" I am a winner, so I keep on winning as it is a part of my life. I deserve all the most refined things this world has to offer.

- When I set a goal for myself, I act as if it has already happened. I speak about everything in the present tense. I am a billionaire, so I will do what a billionaire does and deserves (even though I might not be a billionaire yet, I will still act and speak like one, and eventually, I will speak it into existence).

Chapter 4: Visualization

The morning ritual gives me an abundance of peace, a sense of control, and a clear mind to start the day. Once I am finished with my CRM and affirmation, then I plan my day. I always start with my end goal in mind and work backward. For example, if I want to sign a business contract with a customer, I would close my eyes and visualize shaking hands with him. Both he and I are smiling while we shake hands to close the deal. Then I work backward. What do I have to do to get there? Before I arrive at the customer's door, I need to draw up a contract and proposal. Before I can make my proposal, I need to find out what the customers' needs are and what they are paying for their existing service. What do I need to do now to find that information? I need to talk to their sales manager to find out what issue he is having with the existing vendor. And why would their sales manager want to speak to me? Well, maybe I can bring him some Starbucks coffee and some donuts. No one is going to turn donuts away! Once you start at the end and work backward, everything is easy to do. No problem! Just put those steps in your calendar and execute them one at a time. Then voila, you've got yourself a deal!

The most important part of the whole process is Visualization. Our brains can't tell what is real and what is fake. Thus, many things can be *spoken into existence*. For example, if I visualize that a particular meeting with a customer will end with an order, it will happen. I simply need to think about it, talk about it, and act as if it has already happened, and it will happen. It is the strangest thing, and I am not a religious person, but once I visualize my goal, it seems like everyone is there to help me achieve it. It's simply a fantastic feeling. We will discuss this in detail in a later chapter.

Now that you know exactly what you need to do to achieve your goals, do the following before leaving your house for work or school.

1) Look at yourself in the mirror and laugh nonstop for 3 minutes. There doesn't need to be a reason. My brain does not care why I am laughing, but it is happy when chemicals such as dopamine and serotonin rush into my brain.

2) Look into the mirror again, gaze into your own eyes and say, "Self, I love you. You are the best at what you do, you are a kind and loving person, and you are a successful person. Now go out, say hello and smile at everyone I meet, and see what I can do to serve others."

3) Close your eyes and visualize your day going perfectly: getting the deal you need, having a loving moment with loved ones, getting whatever you set out to do done perfectly and easily. Then open your eyes and do three big fit pumps while yelling, "Yes, Yes, Yes, Thank you, Thank you, Thank you!"

Now you are ready for the day!

Chapter 5: Positive Reminder

People have asked me to identify the number one thing that a person needs to do to become financially successful. The answer is simple: self-discipline. The definition of self-discipline is doing something even when you don't feel like doing it. It is not easy to be self-disciplined. To help me, I programmed my iPhone calendar to remind me every day that I need to do my CRM first thing in the morning. I call it my morning PR, or positive reminder.

Sometimes I get lazy when I wake up in the morning, and the thought of skipping my CRM crosses my mind. Immediately I read my PR, or my Positive Reminder, to remind myself why I want to do my CRM in the first place. This reminder gets my mind straight, and I'm able to start doing what I am supposed to. Nobody is perfect, and everyone needs a reminder or a kick in the behind sometimes. My PR is that kick. Below is a list of reminders on my PR.

1) Willpower is strongest in the early morning, so I must wake up early and do my CRM, speak my daily affirmation out loud, and then visualize my perfect day as if it has already happened.

2) I say to myself, "It's going to be a great, amazing, wonderful day." Then I put my right hand over my heart and take a deep breath. I think of loving moments with my family and loved ones. "What and who

do I appreciate today? Thank You, Thank You, Thank You." And I say my appreciation out loud with a big smile on my face.

3) If I don't make time for health now, I'll have to make time for illness later, so start my CRM NOW. Also, exercise is not all or nothing. For example, I can get on my back on do some crunches when I watch TV. Every little bit counts when it comes to one's health.

4) Follow the 5-second *"Just Do It"* rule. When I wake up and open my eyes, I get up, make my bed, say three thankful things, brush my teeth, and start my cardio. Once I get started, which is often the most challenging part, everything that follows gets easier. Everything becomes automatic once habits have formed. Cardio is followed by Reading and then Meditation.

5) Doing my CRM and Affirmation gets me in a positive, happy, and grateful state and helps me to focus on the right things. When I do my meditation, I can also think of the people I love the most in this world and of all the wonderful times we have had together. Even if they are not in this world right now, they are in my heart supporting & accompanying me. I can use meditation to zoom in on love and zoom out on challenges. Notice I did not use the word issues or problems. Instead, I use the word challenges because a challenge is something that I can overcome and learn from. Using positive words is very important.

6) Do not touch or even use your phone until you are finished with your CRM and Affirmation. This is very important. I usually put my iPhone on Airplane mode the night before, so I don't get any notifications or disturbances. Nothing is more important than completing this ritual every morning.

Jason A. Scott

Head High Chin Up Winning Positive Morning Ritual

Mission: Positive+Gratitude ➔ Happy ➔ Success ⬅ More Experience
(My Choice) (My Choice: Im responsible for my own only) Growth Learning

Purpose: I believe everyone has right to decent living by having roof over their head and ability to eat healthy food. I help the underprivileged finding housing for their families, and help seniors live a healthier life with better teeth.
Mission: Life always go in a full circle, the only true happiness is be with the ones I love, and I only do what makes me happy by living & loving the life I choose. Simple Routine Life = Best Life. I choose to be happy 24/7 & bring happiness to everyone around me. I'm GRATEFUL and APPRECIATE all the simple things and experiences. I'm living an amazing life w/ positive attitude. I am on top of the world Today & every day. I can see goal right in front of me. I'm simply unstoppable. I'm so glad to be alive and I'm going for it 100%, nothing can hold me back. NOT A THING! My name is Jason & I drink lots of water & workout every day! I keep myself in good shape mentally & physically so I look good & feel great & keep on winning. I love my morning ritual because I love how it make me feel

- I am happy (BIG SMILE)
- I am positive, smiling, laughing (self/stranger)
- I am healthy (160 looks) my youth face fit body,flat ab)
- I am super smart & filled w/ energy
- I am focused (where energy will flow)
- I am efficient & productive
- I am responsible, what can I do now?
- I am calmed & relaxed as peace of mind is crown jewel of wisdom
- I am always confident & prepared
- I am thoughtful & considerate
- I am grateful (replace expectation w/appreciation)
- I am self-discipline, loved, think, abundance
- I choose deferred gratification over instant reward
- I am resourceful, always in control of my own destiny
- I dictate my own path & future reality
- I slow down and enjoy the moment
- I live & breathe positive energy living every moment in life "Life is good, life is easy, all good things come to me"
- I do "The One Thing" to get 80% results w/ 20% effort
- I don't worry because it doesn't achieve anything
- I can't stress about things out of my control
- I turn everything into positive by changing how I look at them. Traffic & fine give me time to relax & think
- I am a winner so I keep on winning as it's part of my life. I expect to be treated the best to get the best, "why not me and why not now?" Act as if...billionaire

Daily Ritual

- Gateway to daily energy - moment to relax, breathe deeply, drink H2O, slow food, visualize fit body when exercise, focus on how I feel when in nature, be fully present now, altruism, OneNess – time in nature, see hear feel with blank head
- Turn – turn difficult experience by replaying it as if it went perfectly, then focus on future wants and feeling as if I am getting it already
- Deliberate daily good deed, Daily Magic Moment Board. Positive Thinking 24/7, Minimize choices keeping WP
- Happy Words Only 24/7 - enjoying, joyfully, happily, proudly, delight, lovingly, enthusiastically, thank you. Hangout w/ only happy people
- What's most productive thing I can do right now? Do-Repeat, "Do" instead of "Complaining". Plan 4 worst, hope 4 best
- Low Info Diet: read w/ purpose, learn from each experience
- Look for patterns so I can systemize
- Amazing people is everywhere, I just need to start w/ "hello", SWSWSW: some will, some wouldn't, so what! Act as if it's already one, speak everything in present tense.
- Do Not stress over little things, they are All little things. Do I want to be right or do I want to be happy?
- Time - priceless so don't ever waste it, only spend it with ones I love and things I enjoy. Associate w/ positive winners, rid of destructive losers even family member
- Laugh when I can, apologize when I wrong, let go of what I can't change
- Daily Charity - over tip, brighten someone else's day, compliment, act of generosity/kindness
- Recognize Fear & Angry, then focus on what I can do now (only action yields results)
- Stay away 5 White Poison: sugar,salt,flour,bad sleep,negativity

Food

- Grocery from list: no junk food/processed, whole food, protein chicken, gallon h2o
- what I eat/drink/ breathe today = my cell tomorrow
- Stay away from stress,anger,sadness,boredom
- No Reading while eating,live the moment; use all 6 sense to enjoy heavenly food

Friends

- Listening, complimenting, agreeable,cheerful, raise others self-steem. Be interested instead of be interesting. Ask questions so they can talk about themselves. Positive
- Asshole: bragging, change subject to self, lying, don't say hello or make eyes contacts
- No unsolicited advice. I don't give answers, I just ask good questions
- Woman: 3 Second Rule
- Woman Pure Spinning: imagination, competition anxiety act implied non exclusivity is the key. I communicate mysteriously with my behavior so she can draw her own conclusion. Alpha/Beta, Sunday Pancake story.

Hot

- Feedbacks: "Hey, would you rate me as a manager on scale 1-10?" "what would it take to make it a 10?". "Thanks for caring enough to share this with me"
- Listen: eye contacts, body language, ask for clarification, which triggers message. SAL: Only learn truth or if it come back 10X more & me worrying less
- "How do you see this... now it's your plan to resolve this, how do we follow up?"
- "I can't help but noticing you don't look like you're in a really good space... I'm really concerned. Or "you don't look happy. What's going on? What I don't know I can't fix. Peace & Respect - first & #1 requester at work. Sandwich method. "You know.. you are a really good friend"
- I hope you made the best decision. Always stand do it

Morning Ritual <strongest Will-Power in early morning>

< It's going to be a great day, hand to heart breathing & think of loving moments. whom do I appreciate today? Thank You Thank You Thank You w/ big smile >
< If I don't make time for health NOW, I'll have to make time for illness >

1) 5 second rule "just do it" wake up, brush,cloth weight
2) Positive happy grateful state, wonderful years even now she's in my heart expecting & accompanying me
3) Stretch(shoulder turning, towel, push/pull back to wall; ankle kneel turnbomb? blank, ab+chest, back roller
4) 3 min laugh, Relax 5 min meditate or Robbins Morning 2 step
5) 30 min Smile Cardio / Road / Outdoor
6) Day Planning, Goal achieved w/ Detailed Visualization to Reality & Memory Visualize positive Energy in my head w/ shredded body <BIG YES PUMP>
7) Hot H2O med, out by 7:30 back by 8:30, then gym read section

GOAL 2019 <baby step, zomo circle, defend boredom w/OT, Swim, Park, Tennis Read Learn>

- Healthy physique 165, 15 min food delay, eat all/nothing exercise, sit down day a sun recovery day.
- Daily Magic Moment of Appreciation: Love of family/friends/iphone as simple things
- Daily 5 complimenting & thanking others to brighten their day beginning at their names. Morning Huddle sharing good things, Daily Charity
- Travel to 5 new destinations w/happiness anticipation
- STM: k70, LTM: M12 by 12/2020
- Timeline Jan-Apr ; Fit, Auto Pilot May-Aug New Apr Sep-Dec EOY Goal

Simple Principle of Life & Finance

- Law of Attraction: I get what I think/give, eg body,health,love $, act as if it has already happened.
- I control my reaction, own thoughts 100%, turn negative to positive immediately. Quick Shifter Technique: image of beautiful chournama, 60s music, switzerland nature, tubing trip. "What can I do now? What can I learn from this?" ZoomIn ZoomOut Technique. Accept truth, never in denial, attack concern head on NOW.
- Resentment: 10 d ("I'm angry at. I feel sad that...", don't let it live win me rent free. attack it w/ 10+ appreciation "but", so I can release the past, move forward future. Thank them for lesson. Outside environment = a reflection of my attitudes & expectations, which I have complete control
- Murphy's Law: Anything that can go wrong will go wrong, always trust own instinct
- Go w/ instinct when lots of factors or important decision eg: career, choose mate
- Never give up leverage until I get what I want. eg 2019; Think logic with emotion, think long term, no one control my destiny
- Don't waste a second dwelling on negative thoughts, get up immediately to move back to positive cycle. Power of positive mental attitude. "There's a problem, that's good!" Use bird-eye perspective, not bug-eye
- See good in everyone, situation. Best scenario- tip ahead & eat expectation
- Long term success – gain good habit by bypassing using willpower, instead create a system or put my laziness as a tool
- Act now to deal w/concern head on or let it go, don't give it power over me, 92% of worries never happen; Action brings confidence, inaction brings fear; When there's doubt, there's no doubt
- Act now on Opportunities that makes sense "Ted William Hitting Map"
- Short Term Loan: something I can pay back within a year. New investment can NEVER jeopardize existing investment
- Best deal is one that didn't happen, better deal is usually right around corner
- Buffett: to be fearful when others are greedy & greedy when others are fearful
- Spend time thinking it thru, once decided, act w/ lightening speed 80/20. Spend time to think, most people rather tear pain than to think, trying to stay above water
- Happy Money, focus on abundance, inner joy, inner peace. Spend more happy $, feeling happy now and then massive $ will come automatically.
- Selective forgetting is the true wisdom, always find reason to feel fortunate
- "No" is a complete sentence and most efficient word. 80/20 Say no to the good so I can say yes to the great
- Key to all happiness - Self-discipline: high self-esteem, high net worth, sophistication and accomplishments; & it make me feel good about myself NOW
- There's nothing either good or bad, but thinking makes it so. Rich talk about idea, Poor talk about people and things.
- Only 2 ways to gain wisdom, learn from my own life or study others
- 3 Motivation: Extrinsic (short time pleasure), Intrinsic (passion winning self growth), Pro-social (higher purpose for others lasting long time)
- Physical Happiness: health & freedom, using personal energy as my atonement (good sleep, diet, exercise)
- Forward Happiness: Being content and living the moment (traveling stop & spend the whole day/week at that moment), future fulfillment of my best potential

- Meeting: "What's the next action?" gives CLARITY & FOCUS
- Meeting: Others talk,be quiet,no expression/words, SPEAK LAST
- Meeting: 1)What's on your mind?2)what else?3)how can I help?
- Meeting: positive, recognition, appreciation, encouragement

Chapter 6: Principle of 80/20

I am sure most of you have heard of the Pareto Principle, or 80/20, rule. In essence, it states that everything in the world falls into percentages of 80% vs. 20%: in work, 80% of the impacts result from 20% of the effort; in business, 80% of the revenue comes from 20% of the customers; in money, 80% of our income results from 20% of the job we do; in wealth, 20% of the population controls 80% of the wealth in the world today. The list goes on and on as the principle is very versatile.

One of the most common contexts for the 80/20 rule is in business. It's often said that 80% of any company's profit is generated by 20% of its customers. So what can you do with this principle? If the vast majority of the income comes from 20% of my customers, I will need to do two things. First, I need to fire 80% of my customers who are not contributing to the bottom line. Then I will use the time I saved to serve the remaining 20% of my customers who make me the big bucks. Understandably the first step, firing your customers, might seem difficult to do. However, it is the right thing to do, and you will end up way ahead in the long run. Businesses should only focus on the vital 20% of activity to maximize efficiency.

Another instance in which the 80/20 principle can be best applied is time management. There are always many things that need to get done. The key is to prioritize. As everyone always seems not to have enough time to do the things they want to do, applying the 80/20 rule here is critical to your success. There are always things to do. But you only want to focus on doing things that will help you generate 80% of your income. One thing I do when I wake up every day is list ten things I need to do that day. Then I put them in order of importance from top to bottom, with the first item being the most important and the last item the least important. Then I select the top three items and put them in my calendar in order of importance, just like below:

8am: Call client A, apologize for the shipping mishap and attempt to get an additional order
9am: Call city hall, get the permit approved
10am: Visit client B, show proposal, and get order confirmed for next year

The key is to do the most important, and usually the most difficult, things first. Once you get Task #1 done, you have the momentum to carry on to your second task. And if Task #1 turns out to be more time-consuming and takes up more of your time, it's OK because you started doing it first, and you will have plenty of time to see that it's done before you move on to the second task. At this point, you might ask what to do with items 4 - 10 on your list. Well, just delete them! Yes, you heard me right, delete those "important things" from your top 10 list. The fact that those seven items did not make your top 3 list tells you that they are not so important after all. Those seven potential "issues or problems" already took care of themselves, and you don't even have to worry about them anymore. Or, if they make it to the top 3 tomorrow, you can deal with them tomorrow. Now that's prioritizing. Another option is to delegate the items on the very bottom of your priority list to others. Since they are not so important, even if you delegate them to someone else and they screw up somehow, it's no big deal.

The key is to do the most important, and usually the most difficult, things first.

Bill Gates said something in his biography that I will never forget. He said, "the world is fair. I wake up every day, having the same amount of time as the next guy." What he said stuck with me, so I never waste a second of my time. I do everything most efficiently and productively. That's how the 80/20 rule impacts everything I do.

In your personal life, on things such as dating, you can also use Pareto Principle. What I am about to say might offend a lot of people, but I decided to include it in my book because I believe many people will benefit, or at least be less confused when it comes to dating. Studies have shown that "the bottom 80% of men (in terms of financial strength) are competing for the bottom 20% of women." Likewise, "the top 80% of women (in terms of youth and beauty) are competing for the top 20% of men." That is why you often hear women saying that all the most eligible men are taken, and they are correct. And for men, there is just absolutely no need to chase after women; just make sure you keep yourself fit, and make a decent living, then just let the 80/20 principle go to work. Everything will take care of itself.

Focusing on a narrow set of the most impactful changes that can be made in your personal and professional life can bring about tremendous improvement. If you carefully apply the 80/20 principle to your life, it will lead to significant progress.

With the 80/20 principle in mind, I highly recommend spending time to develop the following four skills: Communication, Planning, Systematization, and Organization. Once you excel in those four things, you can use 20% of your effort to achieve 80% of your results.

Chapter 7: Principle of 99/1

I have applied the 80/20 rule in everything I do, and it has helped me tremendously. In addition, especially in the past five years, I have taken the 80/20 principle a step further and become a firm believer of the 99/1 rule. In fact, the top 1% of the world's population controls, directly or indirectly, 99% of the money in the world. Even if I am not in the top 1% right now, I will think and act like the top 1% so that I can get there one day. What does that mean to you? It means that the decisions you make or the things you do will differ from those of the vast majority of people. The bottom 99% most likely will not agree with you, or they will even laugh at you, and that's ok. Always trust your gut and do whatever you think is right. It is just a matter of time; you will always end up on top. People often say that it is lonely at the top, and they are exactly right. You are successful or will be successful because you do things differently than others. Most people will be jealous of you or even chastise you, but at the end of the day, you will have more money and possibly more happiness than them.

When I hear criticism from others or listen to someone explaining to me "what they think is the right thing to do," I immediately remind myself that I am making the "1%" decision, so why listen to advice from the 99%? Then I instantly shift from a negative mindset to a positive mindset. For example, during the pandemic, one of my colleagues thought Covid was a hoax and that no one should wear a mask. Later on, the same person was the first one asking for better personal protection equipment! It just blows my mind how a person can be so idiotic and hypocritical.

When you encounter a new challenge, the best thing to do is first find all the facts, analyze them, listen to all suggestions, explore all options, and then use logic to make the best decision you can. Once the decision is made, stick to it, no matter what others, aka the 99%, say. I want to note here that although I usually spend a very long time gathering all the facts and studying them carefully, once a decision is made, I act with lightning speed. I plan out all the action steps I need to take, put them in the correct sequence to save time, and think of all the possible scenarios so I will know how to deal with them when they happen. There will be no surprises when I start executing my plans.

Chapter 8: Learn from History

There are many common English idioms and expressions, and I find them to be true in most cases. Unfortunately, most people, including myself, need to learn that the hard way. I want to share some of my personal experiences and add some modern wisdom to those idioms.

I am sure everyone has heard of Murphy's Law, which states that "Anything that can go wrong will go wrong." In most cases, it is true. My philosophy is to always prepare for the worst and hope for the best. If I think of all the scenarios and am ready for whatever happens, I can rest easy. Whatever life throws at me, it's within my expectations; there won't be any surprises, and I can execute whatever I have planned. The end goal will be successful for whatever I want to accomplish.

My philosophy is to always prepare for the worst and hope for the best.

There is also another saying, "If it's too good to be true, it probably is." This is also very true. There is no free lunch, no matter what. No one is stupid. Nobody is going to offer you freebies and not expect something in return. For example, whenever I shop at a local Costco, I see many vendors offering free samples between the aisles. Indeed, you can easily just take the food, taste it, and then just walk away. But it's human nature to be reciprocal, which means you will feel guilty if you just try the food and walk away. So 50% of the time, people will buy the product to avoid that uncomfortable guilty feeling of "taking advantage" of those vendors handing out samples. That's one of the ways manufacturers get people to buy their products. Another example is free apps online. Some people might think there are many apps online that are free, such as Facebook or Google. Wrong! When you sign up with Facebook, you give them consent to use your information for any purpose. So Facebook collects data about you and your spending habits so they can turn around and sell this data to other people. So if it seems like you are using an online app for free, make no mistake, you are the product.

If it seems like you are using an online app for free, you are the product.

Another idiom you may have heard is "You can't have your cake and eat it too." This one I'm afraid I have to disagree with. I think a person should always expect the best, so they will receive the best. For example, when I go out to eat, I expect to dine at a high-end Michelin restaurant. When I stay at a 5-star hotel, I expect the staff to provide me with impeccable service. When I go on vacations, I expect to try everything that is unique or new. After all, life is all about experiencing new things, and anything new is good. I am here in this world to make a lot of money and have all the finest things. Even if I am not a billionaire yet, I will act as if I already am. I talk and act just like a billionaire and attract everything that's top of the line. And why not? I deserve it! So why can't I have my cake and eat it too? Of course I can! This is the mindset everyone should have no matter where they are in their journey. It does not mean that you should feel entitled; instead, you should work hard so you can get to a place where you receive all the best things this world has to offer and nothing less.

Chapter 9: Travel

Every year, I set a very important goal: traveling to at least five new destinations. It can be anywhere in the world, as long as it's a place I have never been to before. I love seeing new things, new places, and meeting people from different cultures. I like to talk to the locals and try to learn their cultures and sometimes even their languages. It's a fantastic feeling when I can experience a unique culture and learn something from it. That's why travel is such an essential part of my life, as it should be in everyone's life. I know someone who has lived in New York City his whole life and refuses to travel outside of NYC even though he has the financial resources. He thinks that everything he needs is in the city, so why go anywhere else? I have since given up trying to convince him to go on trips with me. Don't be that closed-minded person!

I started traveling around the world when I was young. I used to want to hit as many tourist spots as I could. I thought that seeing as many destinations as possible was the best way to travel. Boy, was I was wrong. I ended up tired and exhausted after those trips instead of relaxed and re-energized. But now, as I grow older and wiser, I do something completely different. If I like a place, I stay there for as long as possible and skip the other destinations. For example, recently, I had the chance to visit Lake Moraine in Banff National Park in Canada. The scenery of the place is simply amazing. It's exactly like what you would see in a picture; it's so beautiful and stunning. I was deeply moved by such an extraordinary scene. So instead of stopping briefly to take some selfies and moving on to my next destination, I spent the whole day there, just sitting and admiring the view. It was one of the best trips of my life, and I will never forget it! The lesson is that whenever you see something you like while you are on a trip, stay and enjoy the moment because something like that is rare, and you might not get the chance to see it again.

Whenever I go on a trip, I spend lots of time planning and ensuring that everything will go smoothly. I google the top ten attractions I would like to see in a particular city, but relax and go with the flow once I arrive at my destination. On the first day, I try to get familiar with the surrounding area and buy some local food/fruits to enjoy, and then I check with the hotel front desk to see what attractions they recommend. On the second day, I start with the top attractions on my list and work my way down. There are times when I only make it to the top 4 attractions on my list, and that's ok. As long as I enjoy myself and live in the moment without feeling rushed, everything is just fine.

When I went to Vienna several years ago, I had 15 places on my list. I ended up just going to the first two: the famous Vienna museums during the day and Mozart concerts in the afternoon. I had so much fun just doing these two things that I just kept doing the same thing over and over again for the whole week. When I got back from my trip and told my friends about it, they all thought I was crazy. But it was one of the best trips ever because I enjoyed what I considered to be the best that Vienna had to offer: learning the history of Europe by visiting the museums and listening to classical music by one of the best composers in the world. At the end of each trip, I ask myself, "what did I like most about this trip?" Whatever the answer might be, it solidifies the experience in my memory, a happy memory I can bring back anytime in the future.

I try getting out into nature as much as possible whenever I go on trips, as this is where I get my rare peace and quiet in this crazy and fast-paced world. I enjoy either the beach or the mountains. I open all my five senses while I soak everything in. Whenever you get the chance to be in nature, pay attention to what you see, hear, feel, smell, and touch. Do not think about work or anything else. Just live in that exact moment. Think to yourself, you are at the precise place where you need to be right now. When it comes to being in nature, I highly recommend Switzerland. Everywhere you look, it is just incredible scenic.

To take it a step further, I once had the idea of taking a month-long vacation abroad. But I was afraid to take such a long trip because I worried about missing work. I never dared to take such a long vacation until I met James. James is someone I met on an internet blog for real estate investors. He's like me, a successful landlord who owns and manages over 300 rental units. We started chatting online, and we hit it off right away because we are both entrepreneurs that started with nothing, and both became very successful in a short amount of time. In addition, we have many similar mindsets on managing our rental businesses. James told me he would go to Italy with his family for three straight months. I was floored! I am thinking to myself, how is that possible? But I know when there is a will, there is a way. So I arranged a 3-month vacation to Asia the very next month and guess what? Not only did everything go smoothly during those three months, but both of my businesses did better when I was away! James is a true inspiration to me. Because of him, I can genuinely say that I am semi-retired now.

When I book reservations for my trips, I usually start the booking at least three months in advance. You might not know this, but studies have shown that people who are ready to go on a trip are happiest between the time they start planning their trip and the time they actually go on the trip. I call this phenomenon "happiness anticipation," and I have often experienced it myself. The building up of anticipation for the trip is often more exciting than the trip itself. Give it a try, and you will be amazed at how well it works!

Chapter 10: Little things matter & Daily Magic Moment

I go to sleep early every night around 9 pm and wake up the following day with tremendous energy. Then I go through my simple CRM, which is the best way to start the day. I consider this particular time, from 5 am to 7 am, the most crucial part of my day. This is also my personal space/time. I would never let anyone or anything take it away from me. This means I never go to bed late the night before, no matter how tempting it is to stay up late and have fun with friends. In addition, before I close my eyes to go to sleep, I visualize everything I will do when I wake up the next day, every morning routine in detail, such as my CRM and affirmations. I have to admit it was challenging at first; I couldn't wake up on time, and I found it difficult to follow through with the routine. I just forced myself to go through with it, and once I had done the same morning rituals for about a week or so, it became a habit. Now I no longer have to use my mental energy or willpower to force myself to wake up early and do my rituals. Having good habits will free up your mind and your time.

Many people are in the habit of checking their phones as soon as they wake up. Then, they start checking their emails and social media and end up wasting their entire morning. That's a big no-no in my book. There are always things you need to do at work, and there are always friends that want to talk to you online, but those are all trivial and inconsequential things that will not help you reach your goals. Think about it. Most of the time, checking your phone will only bring you stress and anxiety. I know it is very tempting to check my cell phone when I wake up, so I make it very difficult to do so by leaving my phone charging downstairs the night before. And it works! I am way too lazy to walk all the way downstairs, so I just do my CRM upstairs instead.

A person only has so much willpower and mental energy, and it is usually highest in the morning. By the end of the day, most of the willpower is completely gone. So it's important to make the most difficult or important decisions in the morning since every decision you have to make will reduce your willpower little by little. Because willpower is so limited, I am very selective about where and how I use it. I only use my mental energy to make important decisions and not for things I consider to be trivial. For example, I only wear black t-shirts and khaki shorts, so I do not need to waste my mental energy trying to decide what to wear every morning. I think Steve Jobs and Mark Zuckerberg do the same thing as they always wear the same clothes in public. The goal is to minimize the number of choices you have to make throughout the day, only use your mind to make crucial decisions, and delegate everything else.

I only wear black t-shirts and khaki shorts, so I don't have to waste my mental energy trying to decide what to wear every morning.

Perform deliberate daily good deeds. It can be something as simple as opening a door for someone or asking someone if they are okay when you see them in distress. Simple kind gestures to others can mean the world to them. It also does not take much effort; it only takes empathy. This is a small world, and we all have a short time in this place we all share. So why not be friendly and kind to each other? It not only makes others happy, it will also make you happy when you are serving others. It is a win-win.

The goal is to minimize the number of choices I have to make throughout the day and only use my mind to make crucial decisions.

Be a constant lookout for Daily Magic Moments. What is a magic moment? It is usually something very simple: a beautiful butterfly flying in front of you, a gorgeous rainbow in the sky, someone helping an older person cross the street, or someone helping another human being in need. All those are magic moments. I have a little notepad I carry with me, and whenever I see a Magic Moment, I write it down. It helps me notice all the beautiful and positive things around me and makes me feel grateful for what I have. So see it, take note of it, and celebrate it as much as possible! In addition to looking out for daily magic moments, you can also perform deliberate daily good deeds yourself. It can be something as simple as opening a door for someone or paying for someone's order behind you in a drive-through line.

In addition to the Magic Moment notepad where I jot down all the magic moments I see, I also have a Gratitude Board where I write down who or what I appreciate that day. It can be anything I am thankful for. For example, I am thankful to wake up this morning and enjoy the fantastic weather outside. I am thankful to have all my friends and family around me who love and care for me. I am thankful that I live in this wonderful community where neighbors watch out for each other. I am thankful for the frontline workers in the grocery stores in this time of pandemic so I can have food on my table. As long as I fill my heart with gratitude, it will not have room for anything negative.

Chapter 11: Daily Wisdom on Life, Time & Money

There are only two ways to gain wisdom: learn from your own life experiences or study the lives of others. Studying others is the least expensive way to learn, but learning from your own mistakes is usually the most effective. For example, imagine if you suffer a significant financial loss due to a mistake you made. Do you think you'll make the same mistake again? Probably not! And why is that? Because you either lost money or wasted a lot of precious time. So you will never make the same mistake again.

Time is the most expensive thing in this world, so I try to systematize everything I can to save as much of it as possible. If a system is implemented correctly, it can be tremendously efficient and time-saving. For example, I set up all my bills to be paid automatically from my bank account at the end of each month, so I don't have to think about it. To ensure I am not overcharged, I always look through my bank statements and credit card bills every 3-4 months to ensure that everything is consistent. Most credit card companies will work with you if you want to dispute a charge within the past three months.

Life is precious, and we have a limited time to enjoy it, so don't waste your time on unimportant things or people. It's essential first to identify what is important to you and then focus most of your time there. If your family is important to you, spend 24/7 with your family. If you love skateboarding, try to make a career out of it so you can do it all the time. Remember, you are doing exactly what you should be doing if you are doing it with a smile on your face. So how do I spend my time? Well, first, I identified what's important to me. It turns out that I genuinely enjoy spending time with my dad and friends, working efficiently, living and breathing in nature instead of in front of a screen, having peace of mind, reading, listening to classical music, feeling grateful toward everyone and everything, and sleeping well. I try to do these things as much as I can!

I live close to a retirement community, and I love listening to older adults telling me their life stories. They have experienced life and have been through it all, with events or people, so they are very wise and observant. I often find brilliant insights on how one should live life just by listening to them. They love telling me their stories, and I love learning from them; it's a win-win.

I know I've had a great day when it feels like a simple, uneventful day at the end of it. All days are good days because my mind makes it so; every moment is terrific because my mind makes it so. Everything is just like breathing. There is no good or bad, just one breath after another. Life goes on, no matter what.

In addition to my daily mediation and annual three-month vacation, I also plan a 1-2 week vacation at the end of every month. I have to admit that when I first started, it was challenging. After all, there are only 30 days in a month, so if I take my vacation from the 16th to the 30th, it only leaves two weeks to work on my two businesses. I told some of my friends about my plan, and they all laughed at me. They all said that there was no way for me to pull this off. That motivated me. I knew that I was the 1% willing to try new things to get the job done. I carefully reviewed every component of my business and identified which required my involvement and which I could delegate. Long story short, I found that I could manage my medical business remotely by setting up protocols with managers to keep me updated by emailing me daily revenues. This way, I can call them right away if I see any issues. As for my real estate rental business, I set up a system where tenants can pay rent online, so I don't have to knock on doors to collect rent in person. In addition, I created a system to fulfill their repair requests with limited involvement on my end. I also have a system that makes it possible for a vacant unit to be turned over quickly and be filled within two weeks after the previous tenants move out. I have been taking monthly vacations for the past six years now, and I have made minor tweaks to my system at least a hundred times. Now both of my businesses are run like a well-oiled machine, even when I am thousands of miles away.

Whenever I spend money, I use the concept of "Happy Money" to only spend money on things that make me happy. For example, I stay within my budget when I pay my car insurance or utility bills, so I keep a tight watch on what I spend there and sometimes even call vendors to negotiate better deals. But when I go out to listen to a classical music concert or go on a trip to Europe, I don't have a budget at all. Taking vacations and trips makes me happy, so I spend all my money on trips because *happy money* should be spent doing happy things. I will go over the concept of happy money in a later chapter.

A helpful tip on buying new things: whenever you have the urge to buy something, never get it right away. Instead, sleep on it. If you wake up the following day and still have the urge to buy the item, go out and get it. This little buffer time gives you time to think to ensure that this is something that you actually need vs. something that you want. In most cases, you will likely realize that you do not need this particular item after all. Most things you want will be useless within a year, which means they are a complete waste of money. Even though I am blessed not to worry too much about money, I would never waste it on something I don't need. When it comes to expenses, scrutinize every single purchase. My lifestyle does not and should not change just because I am financially secure.

Taking vacations and trips makes me happy, so I spend all my money on trips because happy money should be spent doing happy things.

Whenever I buy material things, I always get the best clothes or things since quality trumps everything. Quality things last. Also, I never go for the latest and most trendy products. Of course, there's always something newer, such as the new iPhone, for example, but material things are irrelevant to my internal happiness. Instead, living a simple life provides true happiness. I always tell my friends that the best way to identify a rich person in a crowd is to look at the watch they are wearing or their cell phone. If they are wearing a $10 Casio watch and an old iPhone 5, they are probably a millionaire. And if you see someone wearing a Rolex and carrying the latest iPhone 12, they are most likely swamped with debt.

Time is priceless. Don't ever waste it because this is the only thing that money cannot buy. Only spend it with ones you love and things you enjoy. Associate yourself with positive winners, and get rid of destructive losers, even when they are friends and family. Learn to say no, and set boundaries with others so you can protect your most precious things: time and energy.

Time is priceless. Don't ever waste it because this is the only thing that money cannot buy. Only spend it with ones you love and things you enjoy.

When something happens in the world around us that does not make sense, there is an easy way to figure out what really happened: follow the money. Put yourself in other's shoes and imagine what you would do in the same situation. What is the most short-sighted thing you would do at that very moment? Answer that question, and you will know exactly what happened. Most people, or the 99%, are short-sighted and act based on what will benefit them the most at that very moment. Don't be one of the 99%!

Learn to say no and set boundaries with others so you can protect your most precious things: time and energy.

Chapter 12: Meditation & Making Choices

When meditating, I visualize a place for my mind to escape, my miniature garden where I can use all five senses, touch and feel things around me, smell the flowers, listen to the birds and trees, and taste the air's freshness. I imagine I am out in nature all alone, sitting quietly and just being by myself and taking advantage of the rare opportunity to have a complete connection with nature. Whenever I am in my house, I try to think of my bedroom door as my gateway to relaxation; I either meditate or go to sleep. I try not to do anything else in my bedroom, and TVs and phones are not allowed!

Every word I use affects my mood, so I only use positive, constructive vocabulary and phrases. I choose words of encouragement: beautiful, enthusiastic, happy, intelligent, honest, friendly, kind, determined, confident, innovative, impressive, forgiving, active, tenacious, thoughtful, talented. Also, words of higher values: fulfilled, meaning, fearlessness, purity of mind, gratitude, service and charity to others, acceptance, straightforwardness, truthfulness, perspective, compassion towards all living beings, gentleness, integrity. Notice that happiness and success are not among those values. They are rewards! In addition, I use happy words such as enjoying, joyfully, happily, proudly, delight, lovingly, and thank you.

Only hang out with happy, cheerful people. Everyone has a choice. You can either spend time with genuinely kind and trustworthy people with whom you can speak your mind or people who are constantly down and complain about every little thing. When I meet the latter kind of people, I don't even say a word; I simply walk away. Sometimes, those downers are close family members from whom I cannot walk away. In those cases, I keep my mouth shut and listen to what they have to say or make comments such as "wow, that's interesting." It's pointless to argue. Just find an excuse to walk away from them the first chance you get!

Life experience and intelligence form a person's instinct, so one's instinct is a reliable tool for making quick judgments on an issue. When I need to decide on something, I do the following. If there are many factors involved or it's a life-altering decision, I always go with my gut instinct. An example of this would be when I chose my long-term mate or decided on a job offer. However, if it's something less severe and less involved, I make a pros and cons list and go from there. When I decide to go with one choice over another, I simply say no to the second choice. "No" is both a complete sentence and the most efficient word. Since time is the most expensive and limited resource in the world, you must say no to the good, so you can say yes to the great.

Always be honest with yourself and others; there is no need to cheat or lie. When you lie, you will most likely benefit in the short term but lose in the long term, just like the saying "you win the battle but lose the war." The longer I can stretch my thinking into the future, the richer I will become. Always think of long-term benefits instead of short-term gains.

"No" is both a complete sentence and the most efficient word.

I live in an above-average area. The average household income in my zip code is around 60,000 dollars a year. Since this is a typical middle-class neighborhood, property taxes are relatively low, and I get to live a pretty comfortable life without spending a fortune. Many people ask me why I don't want to move into a more affluent area like Beverly Hills or the Hamptons. I always tell them that it's better to be a big fish in a small pond than a small fish in an ocean. By living in an average area with low living expenses, I get to save a large amount of money every month. In contrast, I probably wouldn't save anything if I lived in a place like Beverly Hills! Let's toss out a number and say that I can save an extra two thousand dollars a month by living where I do. That's an additional 24 thousand dollars a year! It makes a big difference!

Since time is the most expensive and limited resource in the world, you must say no to the good, so you can say yes to the great.

The rich indeed get richer, and the poor get poorer. It doesn't sound fair, but if you look at it closely, you will realize that it is actually fairer than it sounds. Over 80% of the wealth comes from new money that people make from scratch, either through hard work or self-discipline. In the beginning, the income gap between the rich and the poor might not seem so significant, but over time, the rich will build more assets that generate passive income, while the poor, with their 8-5 jobs, will have minimum increases on their salary. So the gap will get bigger and bigger. It's like a group of fish living together in a small pond: the bigger fish will get more food because they are bigger and stronger, and the smaller fish don't want to mess with them, so they get only the leftovers. As time goes on, the bigger fish eat more and get even bigger, and the smaller fish become skinnier and skinnier. It becomes a self-perpetuating cycle. This cycle is fair because you deserve a better salary if you work harder and smarter than others. And if you are an entrepreneur who risked all your savings to start a new company, you deserve all the profits.

I have an abundance mentality, which means I share more with others than I keep for myself. For some reason or another, this means that I also get more back. This world works in a very magical way. If you want more love, you need to give more love first. And if you want more money, you need to give away more money first. You will get what you give away.

I often slow down to see miracles happening around me all day long on the path to success. I try to be grateful for every moment and stop wasting time on trivial things.

This world works in a very magical way. If you want more love, you need to give more love first.

Chapter 13: How the World Operates

One of the major challenges on the path to success is the presence of naysayers. Sometimes even your family members will discourage you from working on your dreams. Yes, they have good intentions, and maybe they want to protect you from getting hurt. But they are just part of that 99% of people I mentioned earlier, and listening to them will only hurt you in the long run. Thus, one of the essential characteristics of a successful person is to be mentally strong. Instead of doing what others say, do what you feel is right. Below are just some of the principles I follow.

1) Everything is mental and 100% under your control. For example, after playing 60 straight minutes in a playoff game, the famous basketball player Lebron James said, "I am not tired because I don't think about it." That's why he is one of the greatest basketball players in the history of the NBA. Lebron might be physically exhausted from playing the game non-stop, but he is mentally tough. He has a strong mind that makes the physical pain bearable. Mind over matter every time.

2) Practice detachment and acceptance. Always remember the saying "it is what it is." When you reached enlightenment, there is no such thing as like or dislike. You see things for what they are. It is what it is!

3) When people think I'm crazy, I'm probably doing something right because I am most likely doing something that the 99% wouldn't do.

4) Life is not fair, so get over it. Go out and do everything you can to better yourself. Then for some magical reason, little by little, that very same life that has never been fair to you gets a little better. And then the more money you have, the better luck you will have. This is just a testament to you controlling your own destiny.

5) When making a life-altering decision, it's best to be alone so you can think clearly without distractions. So practice and become skilled at solitude.

6) As I grow older, I realize that simple living is how everyone should live, and it is easy. All I needed was a subtle shift in my perspective and habits.

7) Be a person others can trust. Be honest with yourself and others, show others genuine respect, be transparent in everything you do, correct wrongs, show loyalty, constantly improve, be responsible, and keep promises.

8) If there is doubt, there is no doubt. When you are at a crossroads, and you have to decide, the best way to move forward is always to pick the honest and straightforward approach.

9) A person's income will never exceed their personal development, so read! You are what you read. Millionaires and billionaires have a particular wealth of knowledge and self-development. If you are neither, that's ok; you just need to get a book and start reading.

10) Whenever I am faced with a challenge, I ask myself three questions: *What can I do? What can I read?* and *Who can I ask?* Carefully thinking about answers to those three questions will help you solve the challenge.

11) The more I know, the less I need to say. Have you ever noticed that the smart ones are the ones who listen? They let the idiots do all the talking and showing off while they just sit back, observing and learning. Don't be that idiot.

12) Use the power of now. My life exists at this very moment. There is no such thing as "someday," there's only today. For people that tell you that they will do certain things "someday," guess what? That "someday" will never come. So stop saying stuff like "I will go to Europe when I retire," or "I'll start eating healthy someday." Instead, don't think, just pack up your luggage and go on that European trip you always wanted. You will never regret living in the moment.

13) Find something positive in every situation. That's the only way to live. This particular "situation" has already happened, so we might as well make the best of it. I focus on "what's right" and let go of "what's wrong." The best manager walks around the office to catch employees doing what's right and tells them, "great job!" Be that manager.

14) Take the time to think. Studies have shown that 99% of people would rather bear pain than think. That's why 1% of the population, people who spend time thinking, control most of the money on earth. So do you want to be that 1% winner or those 99% losers?

15) Internalize the fact that life is not fair. Instead of trying to fight it, try to figure out how everything works, take full responsibility for everything you do, and learn from your mistakes so you don't make the same mistake twice.

16) Set crystal clear goals, and the world will find a way to help you achieve them.

17) Cultivate self-discipline and a positive outlook. One of my favorite movies is The Shawshank Redemption. In the movie, Tim Robbins spends over ten years digging a hole from his jail cell to the outside and crawls through smelly sewer pipes for 2 hours to escape from prison. And he did it without anyone knowing, not even his best buddy in prison, Red, played by Morgan Freeman. This type of effort took an incredible amount of self-discipline and a consistent positive mindset when dealing with adversity, both of which I greatly admire. These are the traits any entrepreneur must hone to become successful.

There's a saying from the movie I will never forget, "Get busy living or get busy dying." You only get a certain amount of time in life, so you are either progressing and bettering yourself, or you are digressing and worsening yourself. The best part is that you get to choose which path you want to take.

Get busy living or get busy dying.

---

18) I constantly try to evaluate myself and become a better person. I realize that what I do when others are not looking defines who I am. Since I am the only person I need to answer to, I always try to do right by others. When dealing with others, I conduct myself with the highest ethics and integrity. I prefer to keep my mouth shut than to lie, and I spend my time trying to serve others.

19) When we realize we have made a mistake, we continue to see it through to the finish just because we have already spent so much time on it. This is called the sunken cost fallacy, and it happens all the time. No matter if it's a new job or a new marriage that's not working out, watch out for the sunken cost fallacy. You cannot un-spend the time or money, so it's better to drop it and move on. How you use your time, energy, money, and talent will determine your wealth and health. Just remember, if it's not working now, it's never going to work. But how do you know when to quit? Just ask yourself two questions: *Is it working? Do I still enjoy it?* If the answer to both is no, then it's time to stop.

20) Two of the best challenges you can face and overcome are Fear and Failure. The surprising fact is that 60% of fears never happen, 20% of fears are out of your control, and only 4% of fears actually happen and cause damage. And failure is the greatest opportunity for you to learn because it allows you to take another step towards success.

21) When trying to learn from a mistake, pay attention to the "why" instead of the "who." This way, you focus on the event and the

solution instead of complaining about the person who caused it. No one can go back in life or time. There is also no going back on the path to success. You need to press on and find a way to move forward.

22) Luck is a combination of four things: preparation, attitude, opportunity, and action.

Failure is the greatest opportunity for you to learn because it allows you to take another step towards success.

Chapter 14: Positive Attitude and Happiness

People ask me why I seem so happy; they say I always have a big smile on my face no matter what. I don't really know how to answer that question. Life is short; I can either live with a positive mindset doing whatever I am doing or be pessimistic and complain about everything and everyone. The choice is easy; I choose the happier, more optimistic route, and so can you. Below are some principles I have learned on being positive.

1) Happiness is the sum of the simple, little things we do every day. It is health, wealth, and the realization of happiness. Success does not lead to happiness. Happiness does not come at the end; it starts at the beginning and continues all along the journey. Your choice of happiness now will lead to success later.

> *Happiness is the sum of the simple, little things we do every day. It is health, wealth, and the realization of happiness.*

2) It's empowering and liberating to take full responsibility for your life and show gratitude and appreciation without blame. Nothing is good or bad but thinking makes it so. I cannot control what happens around me, but I can control how I respond to it.

3) Whenever I feel frustrated because I failed to achieve my goal, I use the "Turn Method" to quickly get rid of my frustration. First, turn a challenging experience into a good experience by replaying it as if it went perfectly, focusing on what you have learned and how it will go better next time. You can also go a step further, visualize everything in detail as if it has already happened.

4) Do not stress over little things, and they are *all* little things. For example, let's say you will live to be 80 years old; that's 29200 days, or 700,800 hours, or 42 million minutes. Having that in mind, everything that's happening around you now seems trivial. So why stress over them? It's not that big of a deal. There's no need to get mad or emotional about it. Just take care of it and move on.

Do not stress over little things, and they are all little things.

---

5) Do you want to be right or be happy? There is no need to argue with anyone. Understand that everyone has a different level of perception. Even if you know you are right, it's not your job to try to convince someone else to think as you do. Who are you to correct someone else's mistakes, especially if they did not ask for your help or opinion? Keep your mouth shut and mind your own business.

Do you want to be right or be happy?

---

6) Selective forgetting is true wisdom. Always find a reason to feel fortunate.

7) Things happen. There is no need to get overly happy or upset about them. Everything goes in a cycle. Life is similar to the financial market; there will always be ups and downs. Stocks go up and down, just like finance and fortune. But eventually, everything evens out in the long

run. There is simply no need to overreact to something that's most likely temporary.

8) You are what you think. All your thoughts depend on your attitude, whether it be positive or negative. You also have complete control over what attitude you decide to "wear" every day, just like you have complete control over what clothes you pick out. When you direct your thoughts and control your emotions, you will create your own destiny. Always see yourself in the best light: successful and feeling great about everything at every moment. Visualize the successful, positive image of yourself at all times. When you do that, your subconscious will help you talk and behave accordingly, presenting the best part of yourself to the world.

9) Always try to live on your own terms. Happiness is not possible if you can't be yourself. Ever since I was a little boy, I have always preferred to do the exact opposite of social expectation. Call me a rebel if you want, but I have no regrets. I am successful now, and most importantly, I achieved that success on my terms. And that makes me happy.

10) Share your experiences with others. I love teaching other people what I have learned throughout the years and what has made me successful. That's the main reason I am writing this book! The way I look at it, the more I share with others, the more I learn, so I am never stingy when it comes to sharing knowledge. I also understand that the key to success is execution. So many people have ideas, but only 1% follow through and execute those ideas. That's what separates winners from losers.

11) Luck plays a part in every success story. It might be the right timing, or someone may just happen to be there to help you exactly when you need it. But luck can't do all the heavy lifting; you also have to be prepared for when that luck comes. When opportunities come knocking, they will not wait for you. Either you are ready and can jump on the opportunity train, or it will pass you by and never look back. For example, let's say there is an opportunity for me to purchase an

underperforming asset. If I am not prepared (aka have not saved up enough for a down payment), I won't be able to take advantage of that opportunity. There is a saying, "luck happens when opportunity meets preparation." I am often the luckiest person because I am organized and prepared all the time, so when the "opportunity train" comes along, I can hop right on for the ride.

12) Live a life with no regrets as if you won't get to see tomorrow. Since I have lived every day to the fullest, I have no regrets. Whatever you value the most should be where you spend the most of your time and money, so why would you spend more time at work than with your family?

13) Stress is not what happens to you; it is your reaction to what happens to you. If you can control your reaction by simply changing your attitude, then you can control your stress level.

14) Don't waste a second dwelling on negative thoughts. Instead, get up immediately and move back to the positive cycle. Cultivate a positive mental attitude 24 hours a day and seven days a week. When there's a challenge, that's good! It allows you to learn something new and grow as a person. Nothing is better and more fun than learning something new in life.

Luck happens when opportunity meets preparation.

Chapter 15: Self Discipline & Perspectives

By now, I think you have probably noticed that self-discipline is a major deciding factor for success in this world. Also, everything that happens around you can be either good or bad, depending on your attitude. In this chapter, I want to share some principles I have learned regarding self-discipline and proper perspective.

1) If you maintain simple, healthy daily rituals and do those same little things repeatedly over time, then it's very likely you will succeed. Doing the little things can be boring since you don't see any results or drastic changes right away, but it's very effective over time.

2) Sometimes, when I wake up in the morning, I want to be lazy and stay in bed, skipping my morning ritual and CRM. But I always remember the saying, "What is easy to do is easy not to do," as well as the fact I am not the 99%. That gives me the motivation I need to use my 5-second rule and jump out of bed. Find what motivation works for you. Having this kind of attitude will have a snowball effect because your greatest successes in life come from your disciplined effort to do easy things that are easy not to do! You must suffer one of two pains in your lifetime: the pain of discipline or the pain of regret. Which pain would you rather have?

3) In the animal kingdom, birds have excellent vision, so they get to see pretty far, whereas bugs have poor vision, so they only see things that

are close to them. Therefore, when dealing with a difficult situation or a challenge, I use this metaphor to explain the importance of having a birds-eye perspective to see and analyze a challenge instead of a bug-eye one.

4) The actor Will Smith is probably one of the smartest actors today. Something he said stuck with me. He said, "on the other side of fear is freedom." That is so true! If you intentionally do whatever you fear the most, it will be over and won't be a big deal anymore. You will have conquered your fear and will no longer be afraid. You will also gain courage from conquering this fear and become more self-confident. So always embrace fear because the other side of fear is exactly what you need: the reward of freedom. Remind yourself that whatever you are afraid to do is exactly what you need to do right now. Don't wait. Apply the five-second rule and just do it. Almost every time, you will be better off conquering your fear than running away from it.

On the other side of fear is freedom.

5) See good in everything and everyone. That's part of staying in a positive cycle. And in some cases, if you have to take a financial loss because you overly trusted someone, that's ok. Sometimes it costs you a little money to get to learn an important lesson about another person. For example, I once invested some money with a new acquaintance. He ended up taking my money and running when the business went south not too long after we got started. I lost about fifty thousand dollars, but I was not as upset as I could have been. The way I look at it, from a bird-eyes perspective, I could have lost more money if the business had done well in the beginning because I would have ended up investing even more money into it over time. So the fact that this person stole money from me right off the bat was a blessing in disguise! Now I knew the true measure of this person, and it only cost me 50k. That is not a bad deal after all.

Chapter 16: Rules of Life

I have learned many rules from past experiences; I call them "Rules of Life." I have paid significantly to learn those rules, and I wish I had a mentor around back then who could have pointed out all the traps. Luckily for you guys, I wrote down all those rules, and I have lived by them religiously. Now I would like to share them with you.

1) Law of Attraction: You get what you focus on and think about. If you are constantly thinking about meeting your goals and overcoming challenges, it will happen. You will get the breaks. The right people will come along, and you will feel like the world is helping you along the way. So you need to nurture that faith and keep going.

2) To bring about change, you must first change the internal and then change the external. This means that if you want to make a change for yourself, whether it's to achieve a better financial goal or lose weight, for example, you need to change your attitude and outlook first, and then everything outside will follow. If you are having trouble losing weight, ask yourself why you want to lose weight in the first place. If the why or the cause is compelling enough, you will follow through and do it. Suppose a father wants to lose weight so he can live long enough to watch his daughter grow up and get married. In that case, he has an enormously compelling reason to want to go for a run even when it's raining outside. As you can see, when you want to do something, you must sit down and figure out exactly why you want to do it first instead of acting on an impulse that won't last.

3) You can't control what happens to you, but you can control how you react to it. When something bad happens, try not to use your emotions to respond to the situation. Instead, take a deep breath and try to think of a way to turn the situation into something positive. It's all about figuring out "what I can do right now" and not complaining about the situation. I also use the "Quick Shifter Technique" when I get hit with a bad situation. One of my favorite European cities is Vienna, where I often go to listen to Mozart concerts. When something bad happens in my life, I close my eyes and visualize myself in the middle of Vienna, listening to Mozart Opera. Instantly I am happy and positive again. Once again, staying pessimistic will not do you any favors, so instead, keep asking yourself the right questions, such as "What can I do now? What can I learn from this?". Or use the Zoom In Zoom Out Technique, where you zoom in on the solution and zoom out on the challenges.

4) Rich people talk about ideas; poor people talk about people and things. Wealthy people talk about history, the latest technology trends, new opportunities, and investment ideas. They talk about things that can bring them more wealth and happiness. In contrast, poor people are busy gossiping about other people or complaining about something that has happened to them.

5) When you feel something is not quite right in your gut, watch out! Your instincts are trying to tell you something. If there's inconsistency around you, your internal rationalization is most likely trying to blind you and your subconscious. Stop everything and think things through before proceeding any further with whatever you are doing. The best decisions are usually made when you study all the facts and analyze the situation using only reason and logic. If things are consistent with your gut instincts, go ahead and move forward.

6) On your path to success, there might be bumps in the road or a steep mountain to climb. Expect it to be a lonely road, and also expect to be alone during the climb. There is no friend more loyal to you than your positive thoughts and growing wealth. It's also lonely at the top because no one can understand all the hard work and self-discipline it

took to get there. That's why it's important to recognize the power of solitude and treasure all the friendships you have.

7) As I get older, I realize that material things no longer make me happy. Instead, it's life experiences that make me happy. That's why I have done so much traveling and have had many unique experiences as a result. I do not want to be on my deathbed wishing I had done something different when I was younger. You can't take money with you when you die, but memories stay with you forever. Happy memories such as spending time with loved ones or overlooking beautiful vistas are just unforgettable. As I have mentioned before, I am happy all the time because I can choose to be happy anytime and anywhere. How do I do that? Well, it's easy! When I have many "happy experiences," I can just check them out from my memory bank anytime I feel depressed or sad. I can simply close my eyes and think back to when I was hiking in the Swiss Alpes, watching the beautiful Lucerne Lake from the top of the mountain, or walking next to those cows with Treichel around their big necks. That instantly brings a big smile to my face. When I open my eyes again, whatever challenge I was facing doesn't seem so bad anymore, and I can deal with it in a calmer manner and a clearer head.

Rich people talk about ideas; poor people talk about people and things.

---

8) Who you are as a person is who you will attract. Always be honest and do the right thing. This way, you will always attract the most ethical people. Warren Buffet said that he looks for the three I's when hiring someone: Integrity, Intelligence, and Initiative, in that particular order.

9) Life is short, so do whatever makes you happy instead of living someone else's life.

10) Whatever I learn, I want to teach to others. That's why I wrote this book. And whatever I earn, I want to give away.

11) The rich spend 90% of their time planning and 10% of their time executing. The poor do the exact opposite. Therefore, thinking things through and planning carefully will make the execution much more effortless.

12) Mistakes that happen once can never happen again because if they happen twice, they will surely happen a third time. Therefore, you must learn from your mistakes to ensure they don't repeat themselves.

13) Outside circumstances reflect the state of your mind and inner convictions. It goes back to the point I made before. If you feel happy and lucky inside, you will meet happy people and catch all the lucky breaks. Fix the inside first, and then the outside will fall into place on its own.

14) When it comes to material things, less is more, and simple is good. On the other hand, buying a lot of stuff will add drama and complexity to your life, so think twice before making any new purchases.

15) There are amazing people everywhere ready to meet and help you.; you just need to start with a simple "Hello!" The late Dr. Wayne Dyer once said that everyone should use the SWSWSWSW strategy: "some will, some won't, so what, someone is waiting!" So go out and meet someone new every day. What is the worst that can happen when you say hello to a stranger? They can ignore you, and you would just keep walking. There's nothing to lose! Most of the time, that stranger will smile and say hello back. They might even stop and chat with you, and all of a sudden, you have the potential to make a new friend. Or your smile and hello might have just made their day. There are so many more pros than cons. So why not do it? "Hello!"

16) When there is doubt, there is no doubt. If you don't feel completely aligned with something, trust your gut and don't do it. There is nothing you are missing out on.

"Some will, some won't, so what, someone is waiting!"

Chapter 17: Gratitude & Motivation

There will be many ups and downs in one's life. It's easy to get caught up in emotions and get upset or frustrated by the little bumps in the road. One thing I recommend is to practice having a mindset of gratitude all the time. When you are thankful for very little things happening in the present and grateful for everything that has happened in the past, you are thinking positively, and then you can't help but be happy and content with your life right now. Your attitude at any given time determines how happy you are, and you are in full control of your attitude. Everything that happens is happening for a reason; either you can sit there and complain about it all day and get nothing out of it, or you can be grateful that it's a learning experience and learn from it. There are always takeaways from everything experience, good or bad.

Be thankful for everything in the past and constantly search for the additional blessings you might enjoy in the future. Constant gratitude and a positive mindset are the keys to happy living. Some of you might ask, why would you be grateful for someone that has done you wrong? Or someone who is harming your current lifestyle. An example would be someone cutting you off on the freeway and proceeding to roll down the window to give you the middle finger. How would you react to that? It would be a lot easier just to roll down your window and return the favor by either cursing at them or giving the finger in return. That's how 99% of people in the world would react since people tend to respond with emotional outbursts in the heat of the moment. If you choose to go that route, heaven knows what will happen;

there are road rage incidents every day, and you might fall victim to it. If the other person pulls out a gun, it's just not going to end well. As Arthur C Clarke said in the Foundation Trilogy: "Violence is the last refuge of the incompetent." Or you can choose the high road and kill them with kindness by nodding and smiling back at them. That would give them nothing to go on. Maybe they are just having a bad day, or maybe they are in a hurry. It's no big deal in the grand scheme of things. But, of course, it's easier said than done. There's why daily meditation really helps. It helps keep you calm so you can think logically and more clearly, especially in a random moment when you have to make a split-second decision about how to react.

There is absolutely no reason to get all emotional and roused up by anyone, especially by a complete stranger. The above example happened to me a couple of years ago, and I did take the high road and just smiled back at the person. Reflecting on it now, I am glad I did what I did. I also want to thank the guy for being my "personal mental trainer." He and that incident trained me to have better self-discipline, more self-control, and restraint from reacting or acting on emotions. Also, I have learned that living well is the best revenge.

There are four main motivations: love, sex, freedom, and recognition. When I am managing my employees, I always spend a lot of time on training to ensure they are trained well, so they can be confident in themselves when performing a new task. And I praise them right away on a job well done. I also encourage particular behaviors by complimenting them immediately. I have found this to be an excellent way of raising the motivation of people around me.

I am blessed to be able to wake up every day, do what I love, spend time with the ones I love, and travel to places I love. I am also blessed that I am able to continue looking for investments to increase my net worth with assets that automatically generate passive income for me while I sleep.

Having an attitude of gratitude and being motivated to better yourself will make your life fulfilling and satisfying.

Jason A. Scott

Living well is the best revenge.

Chapter 18: Positive Mental Toughness

Energy comes from moving and feeling enthusiastic. Try to act a certain way, and it will eventually become a reality. I always talk loudly and keep a smile in my voice. People around me can sense that happy, positive vibe and want to be around me. Everyone wants to be around people who are positive and make others feel good.

I want to share a story with you. A fisherman took a boat out with his wife to do some crabbing in a nearby sea. He brought a barrel with him to hold all the crabs he was going to catch, but there was no cover on the barrel. The wife asked him where the cover was, and the fisherman just smiled and said nothing. It was a calm day at the sea, perfect weather for crabbing. Within the first 5 minutes, he got a handful of crabs, which he just threw into his big barrel. The wife expected the crabs to climb out of the barrel because there was no cover, but instead, all the crabs stayed put. She was surprised, and so she went to look inside the barrel. She saw that as soon as one of the crabs tried to climb out of the barrel, the other crabs would stop it from doing so. This is a perfect metaphor for most people in the world today! No one wants to see you do well in life; they all want to keep you down so they can commiserate with you on how bad everyone's life is and complain about everything. Misery loves company. Most people like to belittle others and feel superior. Do yourself a favor: don't be that crab! Get out of that barrel as soon as possible and never look back. When I first heard this story, it sounded incredibly cynical. But when I thought about it, I realized it was true. Most people around you would rather see you not succeed. Don't give them the satisfaction! Do well and live well.

The path to success is never easy. The irony is that most of the challenges I faced were from people I knew, sometimes even my own family members. It is essential to be mentally tough and not to be distracted by the negative people around you.

Chapter 19: Power of "Invisible Mentors" & Acting the Part

I rely heavily on both of my "invisible mentors," which are logic and intuition. All the decisions I ever make will need both of their approval. My intuition, or the inner voice, is always correct. When my two mentors disagree about what to do next, I know something is wrong, and I will not take action until I figure out what that is. Sometimes there will be an awkward pause and silence; that's the sign that I need to take a break and give myself and my two mentors time to think.

There are many books written on all sorts of subjects. If there's any field or a new career you want to go into, finding an invisible mentor, aka a good book, should be Step 1. Learning by reading is the best way to gain knowledge of a new topic you are exploring. At some point, once you have finished reading many books on that topic, a human mentor will come along to help you complete that last mile on your path to success. Just have faith and keep on trucking.

Everyone has heard the saying, "fake it until you make it." I am living proof that it works! When I was a college student, I would take my girlfriend to places like Miami for a week-long vacation during spring break. But I was a college student. Not only did I not have any money, I barely had enough to pay for the flight tickets and cheap motels. To have a good time with limited funds, we would go to the five-star Hyatt Resort next door to enjoy their facilities every morning. We would hang out by their fancy pools overlooking the blue Atlantic Ocean. The hotel staff would usually walk around to ensure that everyone using their amenities was a hotel guest, but they never bothered checking me. My girlfriend at the time asked me why they never checked on us. I told her that it was because I always talked, looked, and acted the part. I acted as if I stayed at five-star hotels all the time and looked and talked as though I belonged. It's not hard; simply sound educated when you speak and dress appropriately. I would even throw names of other five-star hotels around to make them think I was a pretty well-off guest. Now, some of you might think that I acted like a con artist. I disagree. I didn't steal, and I didn't lie; I simply acted like I was wealthy, which is not a crime. I got to spend time there and see how rich people lived, and that helped me realize how important money is. I could either work hard and be the 1% and live comfortably like these rich people, or I could be the 99% living life on autopilot and dying with pennies to my name. The choice was easy.

Chapter 20: Goal Setting & Communication

Goals in life should be in the following order: health, wealth, and the realization of happiness. You might notice that I use the same three terms to define happiness. This is because most people's goal is to be happy, so it makes sense.

If you don't have the health to enjoy this precious life, no matter how much money you make in life, it'll all go to waste. Thus, having good health is number one on the list. Wealth is number two. A person needs to achieve financial freedom to enjoy the finest thing in life. Of course, there must be a balance between the two, and you can only do one thing at a time. Should you use your precious time to work out at the gym or make more money at the office? Guess what, if you follow my methodology, you can have the cake and eat it too! Just do what I do: do the 5 am morning ritual and CRM at the beginning of the day, and then you can decide how much time you want to spend on making money with the rest of it. The third goal is a little more difficult to comprehend: the realization of happiness. You will hear other people say things like, "if I can make a million dollars, then I will be happy" or "if I can find the right guy to marry, then I'll be happy." That is incorrect thinking. You are responsible for your own happiness. You! No one else can make you happy if you cannot even make yourself happy. I have realized that happiness is a choice. You can choose to be happy anywhere, anytime. That's the difference between animals and humans: we have a choice, and we control our own thoughts. Once you choose to be happy, your attitude will change, and a miracle will occur: the whole world around you will all seem positive, and everyone you meet will seem cheery and eager to help you. It's a fantastic feeling! Other results of choosing to be happy are simplicity, energy & enthusiasm for life, lasting relationships, emotional and psychological stability, a sense of well-being, and peace of mind.

Anyone can set goals, but it's the execution that is critical to one's success. Winners find ways to make things happen, and losers find excuses for why they failed. Which one do you want to be? The first step toward your goal is the hardest, just like getting out of bed in the morning. Just do it, and you will already have won half the battle.

I learned at a very young age that 99% of communication is non-verbal. Because I have learned so much through reading and observing others, now I can almost predict the future. History repeats itself because most people do not learn from their mistakes. If you want to predict what will happen next, all you have to do is look at history.

Think before you speak. I constantly watch what I say, and I listen to no evil and speak no evil. I try to ask better questions so I can get better answers. Do not ask yourself, "why is this happening to me." Instead, ask yourself, "why is this happening *for* me, and how will it make me a better person?"

Everyone has an opinion, and everyone wants to be heard, but saying whatever we want is not freedom. Freedom is not always feeling the need to speak.

When dealing with grief, it's human nature to go through five stages: denial, anger, bargaining, depression, and acceptance. These five stages are a part of the framework that makes up our learning and enables us to move forward when we lose someone. While there is nothing wrong with that, I suggest that you do your best to move through the five stages as quickly as possible so that you do not become stuck in a negative place. Instead, you need to get back up and get back into a positive cycle. After all, life goes on, and I am sure the loved one you lost would want you to move forward as well so you can live a better life. A friend of mine, Billy, did just that. He lost his mother during the pandemic, and he was understandably devastated. The business he started was also going through a challenging time. Yet, instead of faltering, he rallied and persevered. Although he was overwhelmed by grief when his mom passed, he realized that he still had his whole family counting on him. So he used his sorrow as his motivation. He analyzed his business and came up with a brilliant new strategy to attract more clients. Despite the pandemic, his new marketing campaign worked, and now he's enjoying the fruits of success. I am so happy for him.

Ask yourself, "why is this happening for me, and how will it make me a better person?"

Don't ever try to change losers or downers; just run away from them as fast as you can! It's not your job or responsibility to change their mindsets. They are responsible for their series of bad choices. No one can help them; only they can help themselves. Everyone needs to be accountable for their actions and choices.

Jason A. Scott

People have different levels of perception, so whenever someone has a different opinion than yours and wants to argue, the best response is, "yes, you are right." Leave it at that. Why waste your time trying to correct them, especially when your time is so precious and expensive?

Chapter 21: Dealing with Adversity

There are so many places to get information these days. There are thousands of websites, TV shows, magazines, and podcasts, not to mention emails, YouTube, and newspapers. It's information overload! Instead of wasting time figuring out what's real news and fake news, I stopped watching the news altogether. That's my suggestion to you as well, stop watching the news. Most news nowadays is just there to grab your attention; it's not essential. I bet if you stop watching the news for the whole year, you won't miss anything important.

When something negative happens in my life, I've learned to accept the truth immediately. I strive to never be in denial. Instead, I try to compose myself and spend my time figuring out how to address the concern head-on instead of complaining. Don't judge now; all setbacks are temporary and blessings in disguise, and they can be beneficial in the long run.

Some of the wealthiest people in the world are the unhappiest people in the world. A person might seem to have everything: power, money, time, freedom, but the very fact that they have everything makes them unhappy. You will always want more of what you already have if you do not grasp the concept of "realization of happiness" and contentment. You can access your fulfillment and happiness any time by simply looking inward and finding gratitude.

When I start to feel resentful, I identify the emotion by expressing it out loud: "I'm angry at, I feel sad that, I feel frustrated that…". This way, I don't let the negative feeling live within me rent-free. I then attack the resentment with ten or more appreciations. This way, I can release the past and move toward the future. Finally, I express gratitude for the lesson, as I have learned how not to let it happen to me again. Whenever I accidentally start to complain about someone who has faulted me, I try to catch myself and immediately say one good thing about them. By doing this, I effectively cancel out my previous negative thoughts. Now I am back in my positive cycle. As I mentioned before, it's essential to maintain a positive mindset all the time. Whenever I am positive on the inside, everything will be positive on the outside as well.

One thing I have learned throughout the years is that, generally, the outside environment is a reflection of my attitudes & expectations. If I start to see everything outside negatively, I know there's something wrong within me; my "internal self" is not where it needs to be. At these times, I immediately get myself to a peaceful and quiet place where I can meditate and do some positive thinking to get myself back to the positive cycle. Again, even though I don't have any control over the outside environment, I have complete control over my attitude and responses. You are what you think, so you need to think correctly and positively.

When I start to worry over something, it's just my gut telling me that I am not prepared. For example, if I am worried about a test I'm taking the following day, that means I am not fully prepared and need to study more. I have control over how much time I spend studying, so once I take that step, the worry will go away. But what if the test is more complicated than I thought it would be? Well, that's something that I have no control over, so I should not worry about it at all. Instead, do everything you can about the things you can control and let go of the things you can't.

The outside environment is a reflection of your attitude & expectations.

When faced with challenges (notice I did not use the word 'obstacle' or 'issue' or 'problem'!), I ask myself questions like, "What's the most productive thing I can do right now?" Whatever that thing is, just do it and repeat.

"Doing" instead of "complaining" is the key to success. Be action-oriented instead of passive and pessimistic, which will get you nowhere.

Recognize feelings such as fear and anger by expressing them out loud: "I am angry at him right now because he betrayed my trust," or "I am afraid this deal will fall apart because it will be catastrophic for my business." Once you express the emotion out loud, you have identified what your feelings are. That is crucial! Now, instead of focusing on your hurt feelings, you can instead focus on what you can do to overcome this challenge. Instantly, you turn a negative emotion into positive action, and only action yields results.

When there's a conflict with anyone or anything, first take a moment to look deep into yourself. Once your attitude changes, everything somehow gets resolved. You can control your thoughts and your reactions. Adversity brings out the best in you and helps you mature and build character!

Try to focus on the things you want and desire, not the things you don't want. For example, instead of saying, "I don't want to be poor," say, "how can I reach the next level of wealth?" When you focus on things you want in life instead of things you don't want in life, you reach for abundance. When you have a mindset of abundance, you become a magnet that attracts everything you need in this world. You get what you focus on!

Constantly ask yourself questions like: "What is life trying to teach me now?" "How can I increase my peace of mind?" "What would I enjoy doing to stay strong and healthy?" You will maintain complete control of your life simply by asking yourself empowering questions like these. It's easy to ask empowering questions! "What did I learn from this?" "How can I turn this into a positive now?" Also, always think before speaking. When speaking with someone, wait three seconds after they finish speaking before you respond. By waiting, you give yourself time to think about what they are saying and time to think carefully about your response.

Decisive action cures fear; hesitation and postponement magnify fear. Whenever I see a problem, I always want to deal with it immediately. I spend time doing careful planning, and once I have a well-thought-out plan, I execute it immediately. Everything you do, do confidently and decisively.

Jason A. Scott

What kinds of questions you ask yourself when you lose are important because they will determine how long it will be until you win. Remind yourself that it's just a matter of time until you succeed; it's not a question of if but when! Positive and negative forces are in a constant battle in all of our minds. Whichever you feed will grow, so it's up to you to decide what you want to feel.

Decisive action cures fear; hesitation and postponement magnify fear.

When there's a setback, I simply take a break and do my favorite cardio, usually swimming or running. Almost all the time, the solution will be there waiting for me when I get back. Negative thoughts are like mosquitos; kill them immediately, or else they'll get worse! Use the "Spot-Stop-Swap" method whenever you spot the negative energy: stop it and swap it with positive energy simply by smiling.

I am the first to admit that I have made many mistakes in my life, both personally and professionally. But as long I learn from my mistakes and do not make the same mistakes twice, I can forgive myself and move on. When I do make the same mistake twice, I get upset with myself because it goes against everything I believe in and means that I am not self-disciplined. Sometimes I over-react and stay upset at myself for hours. These are the times when having a good friend is so important. Angle, one of my good friends I have known for years, formed a club with me. It's called the FFF club, which stands for Financial Freaking Free Club. There are only two members in this club: him and me. Even though we are constantly looking out for other potential members to join, so far, we haven't found any like-minded people that we would like to invite. After several years of looking, we gave up trying to find that third member altogether. Whenever I am too down on myself, I call up Angle, and he sets me straight. Once a close family member wronged me, and to make it worse, it wasn't for the first time! I was not upset with him as much as I was with myself for letting this person do this to me twice. Angle said something to me then that I will never forget. He said, "Jason, you need to stop beating yourself up over this. Do you know what he's doing right at this very moment? He's probably celebrating; he probably doesn't even know he hurt you. Either that or he doesn't care, so why are you so upset? The best thing to do now is to forgive him so you can give closure to yourself and move on from this person and move on with your life. Living well is the best revenge." And that's what I did. And now I am a successful entrepreneur, and where is he now? Well, I don't really care.

If there is something negative in the past, purge it from your life and replace it with something positive. Negative thoughts cannot come into your head without your permission. Embrace the difficult things in your life because they are what make you stronger and richer. Whenever you get knocked down, just get back up, take baby steps in the right direction, and before you know it, you will be back on the right path again.

The easiest way to deal with other's disrespect is to talk away from negative people so that you can stay happy while they remain unhappy. There is no reason to get upset, and no one can upset you without my permission. Do not give anyone that permission, not even a family member! With the right frame of mind and time, you will attract the right person and the right things in life.

Chapter 22: Proper Frame of Mind

Every day, there are so many things a person needs to do and so much information to process. There's got to be a better way to "deal" with this complicated world we live in! I try to simplify my day-to-day life by systematizing tasks I need to do and creating routines. My advice to you is to use a "Low Information Diet." Always read with a purpose and keep asking yourself, "what do I want out of this book?". Try to avoid TV News since, most of the time, it's not actually news but someone else's opinion. You are smart enough to form your own views once you gather all the facts. You do not need to listen to some newscaster, most likely part of the 99%, telling you what they think and why you should think the same way as they do. Think for yourself!

The best way to learn is from experience. I meet new people every day from all walks of life; I also see new things happening around me every moment. I try to take in what happened, analyze why and how it happened, and figure out whether I can learn anything from it. If it is helpful for my life or business, I will try to internalize the lesson so that I will know what to do the next time I deal with a similar situation. I also look for patterns, so I can systemize everything I do.

Whenever you encounter a challenge, the quickest way to deal with it is to slow down your breathing, adjust your posture by sitting up straight and exhale deeply to breathe out toxins and negative emotions. This way, you can calm yourself first and get the emotional part of the response out of the way. Then you can think logically and get the obstacles resolved.

I have a saying: "Laugh when you can, apologize when you should, and let go of what you can't change." Life is short, so always take the high road and accept things as they are. Do daily charity. Most of the time, it doesn't even cost anything! Simple, kind gestures like over-tipping or holding the door for someone can and will brighten someone else's day. Sincerely compliment others whenever possible. Always give without expectation of return.

Things will gunk up your mind when you procrastinate, so you might as well do those things at once and get them over with whenever you are worried about something. It is invariably in your best interest to deal with concerns head-on. If you can't deal with something right away, try to let it go, and don't give it power over you. Action brings confidence; inaction brings fear and worry.

"Laugh when you can, apologize when you should, and let go of what you can't change."

Whatever you do, always try to create a better situation for yourself ahead of time. For example, before placing an order in a restaurant, estimate your final bill and tip the waitress in advance. I always give a cash tip upfront and say something like, "Hello there, we are eating here for the first time. I want to tip in advance because I know you will take excellent care of us!" Most of the time, the server responds with a big smile since, now, they don't have to worry about whether they will get a tip at all. My coffee will always be hot, and I know the service will be prompt and friendly. Now that's a win-win.

You are constantly learning as your brain continually absorbs new material from this world, so be ready as new thoughts come to mind. When any ideas about motivations, inspirations, or new learning come along, write them down immediately. When you go home at the end of the day, spend at least a little time thinking those thoughts through and trying to internalize them. It is so exciting to learn new things and improve yourself. Life is a path of progress; if we are not going forward, we are going backward.

There are solutions to all the challenges in life. To find them, you need to use the highest form of intelligence, which is the subconscious section of your mind. This section is accessible when you're meditating, just one of the reasons why meditation is so important! Often, the best time for self-growth occurs when you are practicing your daily meditation. Solutions to life's challenges will come to you when you ask the right questions. Instead of asking, "why is this happening to me?" ask yourself, "how can I turn this challenge into a learning experience? And what can I learn from this experience?"

Even though I am not a psychic, I can predict the future pretty reliably by simply looking at history. Everything is cyclical; it doesn't matter if it's the stock market, economy, war, or human errors. History will keep repeating itself. Use that fact to your advantage, and always be ready to profit from it. What about the timing? Well, when people start saying, "it'll be different this time," you know something is about to happen that has happened many times before.

Act in charitable ways and think good thoughts every minute: smile, respond pleasantly to others, use kind words, appreciate, encourage, compliment, and have positive thoughts. Do this, and you will be rewarded tenfold! When conversing with others, try to use words of gratitude and respect. Terms such as "Please," "Thank you," and "That's wonderful."

Always have a mindset of gratitude. I am so thankful for how lucky I am to have achieved emotional and financial stability at such a young age and to have the rest of my life to enjoy it! Whatever your situation is, find what there is to be thankful for and focus on that. Stop striving and start living in the moment. Live now with abundant gratitude instead of wondering what's coming up next. Doing this will elevate your life's baseline to a permanent state of peace and contentment.

Chapter 23: Habits

As mentioned previously, we all have a limited amount of mental energy and willpower to use each day. Hence, we must conserve our mental energy and only use it to make important decisions. We also want to maintain good habits to do things automatically and don't have to use our willpower on all the little daily choices. Good habits will facilitate your path to success, so why are they so hard to form? Everyone knows that habits like exercising are good for them, but so many people don't exercise regularly. Why is that? Motivation might get you started, but you will need strong willpower to keep you going. This chapter will go over how I reliably form good habits and offer some tips and tricks that might work for you.

Habits can be good or bad. When something is easy to do, a habit is easy to create. So if you want to create a new habit, make it as easy to do as possible. Conversely, if you want to get rid of a habit, make it as difficult to do as possible. For example, to get rid of the bad habit of checking my phone when I first woke up in the morning, I put my phone in another room downstairs the night before. Walking all the way downstairs was too difficult to do first thing in the morning, so voila, habit gone!

Good behavior becomes easy to do when it's repeated to the point that it becomes automatic. Forming a good habit starts with making minor changes in a positive direction; after that, it snowballs. The key to creating a good habit is first to make it easy to do and then just keep doing it until it becomes second nature. A good example is brushing your teeth in the morning: it's easy to do, and since you have been doing it since you were a child, you simply walk toward the bathroom to start brushing your teeth whenever you wake up. It is that simple.

Some habits are a little more challenging to form. One example is the habit of practicing yoga or strength training first thing in the morning. There are several ways to make behaviors like these easy to do: 1) increase your skill level through practice and learning, 2) get the best resources and tools, and 3) start with a scaled-down version of the behavior and then increase it incrementally over time.

Another effective way to form a new habit is to attach it to an existing habit. For example, suppose I already have a habit of stretching my back when I wake up. In that case, I can follow this habit by doing 100 push-ups, and eventually, the push-ups will become a habit too. The old habit works as an anchor to initiate the new habit.

To summarize, when trying to create a new habit, just think of the ABCs: Anchor (having a positive mindset before starting the habit), Behavior (an action that's easy to do), and Celebration (feeling good is the best way to change something!). For example, when I wake up in the morning (Anchor), I jump on my elliptical to do my 30-minute workout (which is easy to do because I put my elliptical next to my bed). Then I celebrate my good habit with a fist bump at the end of the exercise (Celebration).

The single best habit is the habit of appreciation. The first thing I do when I wake up in the morning is to say out loud, "It's going to be a great day, thank you, thank you, thank you." This action immediately puts me in a great mood with a positive attitude and grateful mindset. By doing this, I effectively start the day ahead of everyone else.

Another important habit is the "Negative to Positive Habit." Use a negative anchor to create a positive/healthy response. For example, when someone annoys me, I relax my neck and face and say, "thank you."

Chapter 24: Family

Family challenges are always more complicated than the rest. Families share the same blood and the same shared history and life experiences from growing up. This relationship sometimes makes it hard for me to stick with my principles. Even with the most unreasonable request, it's hard for me to say no to a family member.

Growing up, my mom had very high expectations of me; nothing I did ever satisfied her completely. And my dad always expected me to help all the family members out of a sense of duty, even when they did the most idiotic things. Family drama and difficulties used to give me headaches and bothered me throughout the year. Then one day, I had an epiphany. I realized that I felt responsible for all the grief they caused me because I cared too much about what they thought and said. They had every right to say whatever they wanted, but that did not mean I had to accept it. I was, in a sense, permitting my family members to make me angry. I decided at that point that I would never give them the license to determine my feelings again. Even though they are my family, and I love them, if they create a toxic environment in my life, then I have the right to walk away from the situation or change the topic of discussion. Everyone has the right to their own opinion, and I have the right to walk away and avoid them if I want to. Once I realized that I could deal with my family members the same way I dealt with strangers, my life and relationship with my family improved dramatically. Amen to that!

Most people think they know what's best for the people around them, especially their family members. The family members closest to you will try to give you advice and convince you to live a certain way. Do not let them!

There will be challenges amongst friends and family when you try to live your own life. In fact, this might be one of the most challenging things to overcome on your path to success. Stay focused on your goals, and everything will come right in the end.

Chapter 25: Business

I have started multiple businesses in my life; some have done well, while others have failed. Throughout the process, I learned a lot about what works and what doesn't. I want to share those lessons with you now. Each lesson cost me either a lot of money, energy, or time. My loss is your gain! Before we get started, it's essential to know that every business is brutal, whatever industry you decide to pursue. So it is crucial to keep emotions out of every business decision you make. Think through every decision with the logical side of your brain and not the emotional one!

1) When starting your own business, do not ever go into business with your family. If you do, you will be miserable, and most likely, you will not talk to that person again once the business fails. Similarly, do not go into business with your friends; if you do, the result will be the same. Every partnership ends in the same way, break up. When it comes to money, it's better not to involve anyone you care about. Just like it's not a good idea to mix business with pleasure, it's also not a good idea to mix business with personal relationships. I learned this the hard way. When I first went into business with my mom, everything started hunky-dory. But then she started questioning every single one of my expenses and decisions once we started making money. This was somewhat understandable since, after all, she invested her money into the business and had skin in the game. Still, instead of spending my energy going out and getting us more revenue, I spent most of my precious time explaining every single one of my decisions to her. We fought over every single thing, and it spilled over into our family life too. I ended up buying her out of business, and we

did not talk for several years. No business is worth that! Fortunately, we have since mended the relationship. Looking back, it was foolish for me to go into business with her in the first place; I lost a loving relationship with my mom for eight years over some stupid money. It's just so not worth it.

2) The most challenging part of running a business usually has to do with managing other people. The question every business owner should ask themselves is, "how do I get my point across to my staff so they can be on the same page as me and do what is required?" When I want my staff to correct something they are doing wrong, I use the "sandwich method." It's a 3 step process. First, I compliment them on something they're doing well; second, I point out what I want them to improve on; third, I offer another compliment. This method allows you to begin and end on a positive note. I have found this to be a very effective way to train staff to make changes or corrections. Always remember that people are motivated to change when they feel good, not bad. So use compliments, encouragement, and celebration to encourage that change. It works so much better than yelling or disciplining.

People are motivated to change when they feel good, not bad.

---

3) It's essential that everyone in a company knows the end goal and works together to get there. At my company, we have daily morning meetings where everyone can review the upcoming day together. I like to start the meeting with everyone sharing something positive that happened the day before. It can be anything, perhaps helping a customer solve a problem or something personal like spending quality time with family, just so long as it's positive. This type of positive sharing gets everyone to start the day with the right mindset and vibe, and everything works out better from this point forward.

4) During business negotiations, get everything in writing and never give up leverage until you get what you want. Always think logically and without any extraneous emotion. Think long-term gains over short-term profits! Remember, you will be in this business for the long haul, and if you want to do well, you need to make sound judgments.

5) It's vital to understand the importance of leverage in the world of business. For example, in my line of work, the apartment rental business, I have to borrow money from banks in order to construct apartments. But I am always cautious not to over-leverage or borrow too much. Someone once told me that a short-term loan is one that you can pay back within a year, so it's important not to borrow so much that you can't pay it back within a reasonable amount of time. Remember, the day you have negative cash flow is the day you go out of business. So never put yourself in that dire situation!

6) New investments should never jeopardize existing assets. It's a good idea to create an LLC (limited liability corporation) to keep all your various businesses separate. That way, each business will be shielded from the others' potential losses. That should be the first thing you do when starting a new business. Any competent business attorney or accountant can help you set that up.

7) Remember, one bad deal has the potential to wipe out everything you have made in the past 10+ years. So be careful when making business decisions! Yes, all business involves risk, but you should only take calculated risks. Don't bet the farm on a whim! I am not telling you this to scare you. I simply want to ensure that you carefully think through all the business choices you make because every decision is critical to your company's eventual success. The best deal might be the one that hasn't happened yet. Never regret anything in the past because a better deal is right around the corner most of the time. Once a decision is made, do your best to execute it and move on. If it turns out to be the wrong decision, that's ok, just learn from it and keep going. Never dwell on the past; instead, learn from it and make sure you don't make the same mistake twice.

8) When considering a new business, I spend a significant amount of time thinking it through, sometimes even months. I think about all the planning, logistics, market demands, fulfillment, services, etc., everything I need to do for the business from A to Z. However, once I decide to move forward, I act with lightning speed. Opportunity does not wait for anyone.

9) Whenever a customer tells you "no," just think of it as a delayed "yes." Find out what you can do right at that very moment to turn a no into a yes by simply asking the customer, "what can I do to make you place an order today?" As discussed in the previous chapter, don't be shy. You will never get what you want if you don't ask for it. Persistence is key to success in any business. "No" is just another obstacle before you get to "yes."

10) When dealing with a business crisis, just be honest and truthful to yourself and everyone else involved. Lay everything on the table and decide what to do after considering all the options. Honesty is always the best policy. Take responsibility without any blaming and find a solution to move forward. Always tell the truth and never lie; if you lie once, you will need to use another lie to cover up the first lie. It's just too exhausting and not worth it.

11) I have seen many sales presentations in my life. Most salespeople fail to make a sale because they don't ask for the sale at the end of the presentation. They spend 2 hours making their pitch using great PowerPoint slides that must have taken them hours to put together, but then they don't ask for the order at the end! Why is that? Are they embarrassed to ask for an order, or do they think it's beneath them to ask? I have no idea, but do I know that they just wasted 2+ hours of their own time when they simply could have asked, "so how much of this wonderful product would you like to order?" Yes, it's that simple. This one sentence differentiates the good salespeople from the bad. Ask your customers for the order, and then shut up, give them a chance to say "yes" or "no," and stop saying "no" for them!

Millionaire Success Secrets

12) Business is all about acquiring new customers and getting people to buy a product or service. I wish my first job out of school had been in telemarketing so I could have learned how to sell and, most importantly, how to get used to rejection. Salespeople need thick skins. A study shows that 80% of sales are made after the 5th call, but 80% of salespeople quit after the first call. The ones that quit calling after the first or second call never get over the rejection, and that's why they will never be successful. If I ever have children in the girl or boy scouts, I will encourage them to fundraise by knocking on doors to sell cookies. Watching them get rejected by people initially and then seeing them perfect their sales pitch and reap the rewards would be rewarding for us both. Kids have thick skins, so they make the perfect students. And best of all, they will develop the skills to be successful businesspeople later in life.

13) When you want to convince someone to do something, especially an employee, try persuading them with stories. No one likes to be lectured or told what to do, but everyone enjoys a good story. So tell the person a story, and that way, they can figure out what the moral is for themselves and how it applies to them. Storytelling will both get their attention and make them more receptive to your requests.

14) A successful business should run smoothly without the owner's presence. It's one with an efficient/productive system in place and the right people to run it. If you leave the company for a year, you should come back to an even more robust and healthy business than the one you left.

15) Never market your company as having the product or service with the lowest price. You will end up attracting trouble, and worse, the most disloyal kinds of customers. There's always someone else in a third-world country who can make the exact same product you are for less. You will also notice that the customers who nickel and dime you tend to be the pickiest, requiring more of your time. Instead, find a niche market that fits your specialized products or skills with clients willing to pay more for your products or services.

Jason A. Scott

A successful business should run smoothly without the owner's presence.

16) There are different ways to create new businesses. I like to combine niche knowledge from two different existing industries to create a new service industry that will likely become a profitable business. An example would be an attorney with a medical degree deciding to specialize in malpractice lawsuits. Another would be a nutritionist who also works as a trainer at a gym deciding to open a health food/exercise equipment store. When you have more than one skill or area of expertise, that's where you can make the most money because the idea is unique, and you will have less competition. Another benefit is that you can charge a premium for your services.

17) Hire the best staff and buy the best quality materials; they will give you the best value in the long run. Ensure that every team has the right chemistry; everyone needs to be positive at all times. One bad seed will ruin the team for everyone. My philosophy on human resources is to "hire slowly and fire quickly." I take my time to find the best candidates, but if I see something I don't like and don't think that person will alter their behavior, I fire them immediately instead of wasting more time and energy. Also, when looking for a manager, I try to hire a person with a high EQ so they can babysit those with high IQs. It's good to have a good mix of high EQ and high IQ employees working for you. Since people never change, the best employees are found, not made. Don't waste time training someone to be nice; simply hire nice people.

The best way to teach a skill to someone else is to use what I like to call the "4 step teaching" method. I do a task first, then I do it with the other person watching, then they do it with me watching, and finally, they do it themselves with no one watching. I have found this to be a very effective method when training employees. I also use role-play, where I pretend to be a customer, and my employees try to sell me a product. You can tell a lot about a person when you put them on the spot. I look for people who can think on their feet and make quick adjustments to get the job done.

Don't waste time training someone to be nice; simply hire nice people.

It takes time to run a business. Since my time is expensive, I try to "stay in touch but be out of reach." This means finding staff who can make their own decisions and who don't come running to me over every little thing. The best way to run a successful business is to train staff well and give them the full authority to do their jobs. Sometimes staff members make bad calls, and I end up having to clean up the mess, but that's life. I tell them that it's ok to make mistakes, as long as they don't make the same mistake twice. It's all just part of the learning process.

Best managerial practice - "stay in touch but be out of reach."

Chapter 26: Personal Finance & Attitude Towards Money

In addition to your business, you will also need to manage your personal finances properly to achieve success. You can make six figures every month, but if you don't play your cards right and make smart financial decisions, you will quickly lose all the hard-earned money you just made. The following are some lessons I learned the hard way about managing your personal finances.

1) Anything that depreciates, you are better off leasing. New cars are a perfect example. A brand new car loses 20% of its value when you drive it off the dealer's lot. So if you buy a nice, new vehicle for forty thousand dollars, once you put a single mile on it, you've automatically lost eight thousand dollars. That's why it's better to buy used cars. If you must purchase a new vehicle, just lease it. If you own your own business, you can most likely write it off as a business expense if you use it for business purposes. Consult with your accountant to see what options are available to you.

2) The secret of achieving your goals is to take baby steps. For example, let's say you want to go from Los Angeles to New York, and you don't have a car. You also don't have any money, so you can only get there by walking. It might take you a while to walk all that way, but you will eventually get there as long as you go in the right direction. The key is to be persistent; you can walk 5 miles a day or 50 feet a day, but as long as you take some steps toward your destination, you will get there in the end. I can't emphasize the importance of taking baby steps.

Each step is easy enough, but summed together, they can accomplish quite a lot!

3) I learned the hard way that I should have started my first business earlier in life. When I had a job, I was trading my time, aka my life, for money. When I invest in assets that generate passive income, I am trading my money for more money. Which option sounds better to you? Instead of working for money, my money works for me, even in my sleep! Passive income, which requires no direct use of your time, should always be maximized so you can get to a point where none of your precious time is traded for money. Life is fair; everyone has precisely 24 hours in a day. We use one-third of that time, or eight hours a day, to rest/sleep. If you have a job, counting lunch and commuting, that takes another 10 hours a day. That only leaves you with 6 hours of free time. That is just sad! Instead of working for "the man," everyone should try starting their own company and accumulating enough passive income so they can use their time on more important things, like traveling or spending time with loved ones.

4) No one should know how much money you have, not even your spouse or family. A low profile is the best profile. Don't allow anyone to use that information against you. Unfortunately, we live in a time where some people, instead of being happy for you when you succeed, will be jealous of you and try to knock you down. It is just the reality of things. To say nothing to no one is the best policy when it comes to your net worth.

I am lucky to be in a position where I enjoy doing what I do for a living. It's not about the money anymore. Others ask me why I still work. Well, I love building a business from scratch, improving it, optimizing the model and process, then flipping it at the right time. You can do the same! The only requirement is that you have to get started today.

Jason A. Scott

To say nothing to no one is the best policy when it comes to your net worth.

I have limited memory space, so I don't want to remember or memorize things if I don't need to. If I can write something down, I write it down so I don't have to remember it. For example, if I'm assigned a task, I would go through the following process: 1) is this something that needs to be taken care of at all? If not, just throw it away. 2) if this is something I need to do now? If yes, then can I delegate this to someone else cheaply and easily? If yes, delegate it and follow up later to ensure that it's done. 3) Is this something only I can do, and should I do it now or later? If later, then I'll put it on my calendar to do later. If it's something I need to do right now, I'll just do it, so it's out of my head. Once I am done with it, it's out of my mind completely. Then I can do something else that makes me happy.

As a business owner, I have found the process of making money to be more enjoyable than having money itself. And the money I make now is not for accumulating as wealth because I already have more than enough. Instead, the money I make now is set aside for future investments. It's a never-ending game. But when is it enough? There's a book called "your money or your life." I highly recommend this book for those who are having trouble finding a balance between life and work. This book talks about personal choice. How should you use the limited time you have in this world? Do you want your time to be spent working or doing something else? Of course, everyone chooses what they do at any given moment, but what is the "right" choice? Since time is the most expensive commodity we own, we must be cautious about spending it.

There is constant learning in any business. You need to learn about the latest business trends and also about your competitors. Just like life, running a business is a continuous learning process. The day you stop learning is the day you either die or your business starts to fail. The easiest way to learn something is to listen and then use your own words to teach the new concept to someone else as if they were a 3-year-old.

Millionaire Success Secrets

I try to do most of my work early in the morning because it is the time of least distraction & greatest peace. I am also the most productive and efficient in the early morning. Wake up early to use the strongest willpower to do the most important things, and go to sleep early when there's no willpower left. Since decisions that affect your business or personal finances are some of the most important ones you need to make, make them in the morning when you are at the top of your game.

Often, we don't have all of the information we need to make a decision. The rule of decision making is to not make decisions based on less than 40% or more than 70% of the necessary information. It's better to use your instincts to fill in the other 30%.

You are more likely to retain your wealth if you believe that you deserve it. That's why most lottery winners lose all their winnings within three years. It comes down to how we portray ourselves and what we think we deserve. It becomes a self-fulfilling prophecy. We only attract more of what we already are: health, wealth, and happiness.

There is no easy way to be successful. Not only do you have to work hard, but you also have to be at the right place at the right time. Good timing is the "luck portion" of success. You have virtually no control over it, but you can still be ready for it by being fully prepared. When the timing is right, be the first one to jump on the opportunity. There might be many possible career choices, but I recommend doing the exact opposite of what everyone tells you to do because, chances are, those people are in the 99% group. There is opportunity in everything, even in adversity. Hours of practice and lucky timing can turn adversity into opportunity. This is the type of mentality that every entrepreneur should have! One needs to take charge and be in control of things. Either you run the day, or the day runs you. Either you run the business, or the business runs you. Either you control the relationship, or the relationship controls you.

We only attract more of what we already are: health, wealth, and happiness.

Some people ask me how long it usually takes for someone to become successful. No one has an answer for that, but studies have shown that the magic number for a person to have proper expertise in a skill is ten thousand hours. If you want to be good at a certain skill, simply identify that skill and then put in the hours. One of the world's most famous bands, The Beatles, played in Berlin nightclubs 12 hours per day for one year to get good. Anyone can become an expert on anything if they just put in the time. I have tried to tell everyone I know of this principle. Once I told my ten thousand hours rule to a young businessman, and his response was, "I will try." I just laughed at his reaction. That response really means, "No, I am too lazy to make all that money. I would rather just stay poor." Sometimes, I hear people saying they are "too busy" to spend the time to learn a new skill. I get more excuses from people than people wanting to spend the time to better themselves. For me, I either do something, or I don't; "trying" is for losers.

The wealthiest and most intelligent people in the world often donate large chunks of money and actively participate in charity. Why is that? Well, we can only temporarily enjoy what material possessions we have, but we can enjoy the memory of giving forever. So you will see wealthy people donating to charities, and I strongly encourage you to do the same. That's the secret to long-lasting happiness!

Chapter 27: Obsession to Detail & Watching Expenses

I have been through a lot in my life, and I have also met all sorts of people from all different backgrounds. Those accumulated experiences help me to make very few mistakes now. But I still do make mistakes, of course. Whenever I do, no matter how painful, I am very grateful for the chance to learn from them and better myself so I don't make the same mistake ever again. When you make a mistake, it's essential first to calm yourself and then go through the following steps: 1) identify the mistake and find out why you did what you did, 2) identify what actions you can take at that very moment to either resolve the issue or better your situation, 3) once the challenge is resolved, write down careful notes in your "learning journal" to ensure you do not ever make the same mistake again. Sometimes I see people making the exact same mistakes or bad decisions over and over again. It's like a mouse running on a hamster wheel, and it's just pure insanity.

When it comes to your own company, "good enough" is never enough. Pay attention to every little detail. Constantly ask yourself questions like, "what can I do now to make this a better company?" or "what can I do to offer a better product to my customers?" or "what can I do to ensure my customers receive the product on time?" Remember, every little detail counts. Paying attention to detail takes willpower and mental energy, which are often in limited supply. So be careful where you use your mental energy daily, ensuring you are using it early in the day and only on the most important things. Success is about focusing on a few right things and not trying to do everything.

I used to dwell on the past whenever I make a mistake, feeling the pain as the images of me failing repeatedly played out in my head. Some people refer to this as the toilet bowl syndrome, as the negativity gets worse and worse in a downward spiral. Then one day, I listened to the famous motivational speaker Tony Robbins and learned how to get rid of this bad habit. I added some tweaking of my own and formulated the following method. It is simple but pure genius; I call it the Re-Image technique. Think of the whole failing event from start to finish, then replay it in your head where everything goes perfectly, and then play it over and over again at least five times. This method allows you to replace a bad experience with a good experience! If you replay the good experience in your mind enough times, your brain will no longer know the difference between the two. It will think the good experience is what actually happened. I know you might think I am delusional for purposefully lying to myself about what happened, and you are partially correct. I do this for two reasons: first, as long as I am careful when picking which event I use this reimaging technique on, I will not become delusional. Second, why would I want to keep a painful experience in my head when it only harms me? Isn't it better to just replace it with a fond memory and move on with life?

Success is about focusing on a few right things and not trying to do everything.

There are times when I make a stupid mistake that I want to correct right away. Then I go to a place where I can be alone and yell out loud the word "STOP" five times, close my eyes, then use Re-Image technique to replace the bad memory with a good memory. While I am thinking about the event where everything went perfectly, I do a couple of fist pumps and yell out loud the word "Yes" 5 times. I can't tell you how often this technique has saved me from my own negative thinking and kept me happy all these years.

People start to worry and become pessimistic when they think they are not in control of their lives. It's understandable why people feel that way. We do not have control over many external factors. However, while we can't control what happens around us, we can *completely* control how we react. It's essential to believe that you are in total control of your life and that your response to external factors matters. Your present situation directly results from either a series of good decisions or bad decisions made over time; thus, you are fully responsible and should take ownership of your situation.

As a general rule of thumb, every little thing you do now matters. As I mentioned in the previous chapter, your current situation stems from a series of good or bad decisions you have made along the path we call life. So be friendly, smile, say hello when you walk by people, compliment others, eat healthy, exercise, do positive self-talk daily, and wake up early and do the CRM. By doing all the right things all the time, you are ensuring that you will be on the path to success and happiness. Some people might say that it's exhausting to be friendly even when you don't feel like it. That might be true, but when you're tired, it's essential to "fake it until you make it." On the other hand, when you have a big smile on your face, you can't help but feel good, and when you think positive thoughts, you can't help but feel happy. Results will be there for you as long as you do all the right things, so why not give it a try?

Money has not changed me at all. I am still the same person as I was when I graduated from college twenty years ago. I constantly watch for where I can cut expenses and turn a fixed cost into a variable cost. I understand the fact that the less money I spend, the more money I save. My monthly household expenses have stayed the same even though my income has increased at least tenfold. Warren Buffet, the richest man in the world, says he still uses coupons and never pays retail. When I go shopping, my favorite question for stores is: "Is this the best price you can offer?" And I ask that question whether I'm shopping at a mall or a local mom-and-pop store. There is no shame in being a savvy shopper; the shame would be in spending more than you need to! Just think, if you utter those few words and have the chance to pay less for something, that's the best return on investment you can have.

Success is a journey, not a destination. It is a journey of learning, helping others, and overcoming obstacles. It's often said that the difference between you now and you five years from now is the people you associate with and the books you read. I couldn't agree more. The people around you and the books you read form a considerable part of your life and determine your overall attitude. Your attitude, in turn, determines your actions, and your actions determine your accomplishments. You can see that this is a chain reaction, so every little link matters. For example, imagine there are two boats traveling side by side in the ocean. The first boat turns just slightly left by ten degrees, and the second boat sails straight ahead without turning. You might not see a big difference after a day, but after a week, the first boat will be completely off course and be lost, while the second boat will still be on the correct path to its destination. Every little thing matters, so make sure you don't deviate from your path.

When things happen, I ask myself, "Why did this happen? What can I learn from this? How can I grow from this?" I like to practice Quiet Reflection, where I evaluate every experience I have had and try to turn it into an insight that I can use in the future.

With each decision you make, you are either going up or going down, so be extra careful when making a critical decision. Every little decision you make now can have a snowball effect in the future. It's the small choices that you make every moment of every day that will significantly impact your life. Keep taking baby steps in the right direction, and you will reach your goals.

If you are fortunate enough to own an asset such as an apartment complex that's generating you passive income, don't be in a hurry to pay down your debt. On the other hand, if you own a liability such as a house or a car, pay down your debt down asap. When it comes to cars, always get a second-hand car and never spend more than 20k. Buy something reliable like a Honda Accord or a Toyota Camry. A car gets you from point A to point B, and there is no need to impress your neighbors with a brand new Mercedes. Trying to keep up with the Jones's is a surefire way to go broke. Just as a side note, it costs an average of $9000 a year to own and maintain a car. The average cost of a home pool is around $3000 a season, and a dog will set you back $2000 a year. So think twice before you make those big item purchases.

If you just graduated from college, there is no need to rush into buying a house. Renting might be your best option for a while. Owning a home will cost you more money due to extra expenses such as HOA fees, property taxes, insurance, etc. Most importantly, it limits your options. Since you are just starting out, you don't know where your career will take you, and owning a home might be an unnecessary burden. Renting comes with less responsibility and gives you greater flexibility, allowing you to save up more money.

In life, less is often more. Focus on a few work projects and make them extraordinary. Focus on in-depth traveling to a few select places. Master a few categories of books.

Chapter 28: Health & Zen Moments

As mentioned earlier, happiness requires Health, Wealth, and the Realization of Happiness. Let's discuss in more detail the first and the most important component: health. Everyone is familiar with the basic rules of keeping good health: exercise, eating well, and avoiding the five poisons (sugar, salt, flour, bad sleep, and negativity). While I agree with everything listed above, I also have some additional rules regarding my health. There are two types of health: physical health and mental health. A person must have both to live a good life. I need to be fit both physically and mentally to be on top of my game 24/7, and I can do that by reading, learning, and exercising.

Whenever possible, I like to make my morning automatic, waking up at 5 am and doing my CRM right away before the lazy part of my brain tries to talk me out of it. It is very tempting to stay in bed, especially on a rainy, cold day, but I always make myself jump up and hop on my elliptical. Motivation and the "big why" get me started with this healthy routine, but it's the habits that keep me going.

Daily meditation is so important because it is your opportunity to regain your center and strength. Meditation makes me focus on everyday little things, and those little things are easy to do but even easier not to do. That's where self-discipline comes in. When I first started meditating, I hated it; I thought it was a complete waste of time. But since I promised a good friend of mine that I would try it, I kept my promise and stuck with it. I forced myself to sit there for 15 minutes a day, and after just two weeks, I started reaping the benefits. I was able to concentrate more and focus on essential things. As with any new habit, getting started is the most challenging part; everything else is easy by comparison.

One of my favorite mediation methods I call "Love Meditation." It works like this: step 1) Inhale for 2 seconds, hold, then exhale for 4 seconds; step 2) Imagine the person you love the most in the world sitting in front of you, visualize them smiling and all the details about them; step 3) Allow their love to permeate and radiate through your entire body on each inhale, feeling the love & gratitude in all your cells; step 4) Exhale to release that love like a bright beam of light, blasting the love out to the whole world.

When I do my morning meditation, I try to keep my mind empty. Although there are usually many thoughts crossing my mind when I meditate, I recognize that they are just thoughts and let them flow in and out of my mind without judgment. Then I can just go back to my meditation, connecting my inner self with my outer physical self. At that very moment, I know I have reached the moment of Zen. It is the moment when growth happens, the moment of seclusion and complete relaxation, that illuminates the path forward.

My Zen moment happens when I am self-disciplined and fully engaged in learning. I also define my Zen moment as lifelong learning and continual self-mastery through daily rituals, mental practices, daily gratitude, deep concentration, and focus on the life I want. And what is self-mastery? It is the control of internal focus, emotion, and thoughts, regardless of external conditions.

Sometimes, I miss my morning routine, and my whole day suffers as a result. I make silly mistakes and can't think well at all. When that happens, I know something is wrong, so I stop everything and take a deep breath. I find a quiet place and go through my meditation ritual to restore my usual efficient self before continuing. After experiencing this a few times, I realized just how important my daily mediation was, and I never missed it again. I meditate every day, just like I exercise every day. Even a lousy meditation session is better than no meditation at all! It doesn't have to be all or nothing, don't let perfection be the enemy of the good. Do what you can when you can, and don't judge yourself too harshly when things aren't perfect.

Here are some tips on working efficiently and productively. It's costly when you get distracted while working. It takes an average of 20 minutes or more to get back into focus, so be careful not to get distracted. A phone call or text is often a source of distraction and stress, so put your phone in airplane mode when you are working. Instantly, you are back in control. Sometimes I get behind at work and start thinking negatively. Breathing is a simple and effective solution for many negativities such as stress, pain, and worry. The quickest way to get rid of stress is by regaining control, so take a breath and put your healthy habits to work.

In addition to work, I exercise whenever I can. And guess what, the best kinds of exercise are usually free: walking at a park, hiking, jogging, swimming, or any outdoor activity. Simple things tend to bring more happiness to one's life than complicated or expensive things. Be close to nature, walk barefoot in the grass or sand. It feels completely different, and it's exuberating. When I walk in a park, I walk slowly so that I can enjoy every minute of this amazing world. I use all my senses, feeling how the wind blows at my face, smelling the air and the leaves, seeing the green plants around me, and hearing the birds chirping. Sometimes, I can even taste the moisture in the air. I fully embrace every moment I have on this earth, and it feels lovely. I also love routines. I believe joy is not a to-do list; it's the ability to appreciate and savor the simplicity of each day's rituals.

It takes an average of 20 minutes or more to get back into focus.

I give myself at least 1 hour of "me-time" in nature every afternoon. It can be a walk in the park or a run at a nearby high school track. This is the time to review my day, sweat out all the stresses and toxins in my body, and plan my tomorrow. This is when growth actually takes place as I learn about myself and the world around me.

I used to eat my meals while watching a show or staring at my phone. Then I started intentionally eating in my dining room with my phone turned off. I eat slowly and focus on savoring the food and the experience. I visualize how the food was initially grown by a farmer and all the resources used to ship it to the local market. I take time to appreciate all the people and things that made this happen. Since making this change in my eating ritual, food tastes even more delicious! I know it comes from the hard work of others, which gives me another double dose of happiness. When eating, I chew slowly to enjoy every bit of food. Savor every bite and be grateful for how the food made its way to your plate.

Studies have found that people tend to buy more unhealthy foods if they shop when they are hungry. So avoid going to the store when you are hungry; instead, drink two bottles of water and have a healthy snack before heading out the door.

What types of food should you eat? I try to consume energy-rich foods such as fruits, vegetables, and soy. I also stay away from bread, cereals, meats, dairy, sugar, and alcohol. I also try to avoid watching television and social media and stay away from grumpy and negative people. Remember, take care of both your physical health and your mental health!

When eating, I try to place more value on the consequences and nutritional value of the food than I do on the taste. I always ask myself, "why do I eat this? Is this food going to add to or subtract from my health?" I never eat processed or packaged food; instead, I select whole foods to help fuel my body. Eating smaller portions using willpower alone is not the best approach. Instead, just buy healthy food when you go grocery shopping, and eat as much as you want!

What you do in your free time is a major factor in your future success. Simple pleasures & a healthy morning routine will bring happiness to your life. I do my CRM when I first wake up and then go for a walk in the park to be close to nature. By 8 am, I am already finished with all of the most important things of the day! My day is already fulfilled no matter what I do for the rest of it. If I decide to go to work, I will use the 80/20 principle and only focus on using all my effort on the 20% of tasks that will impact my business the most.

At the end of every year, I sit down and review my goals from the previous year to see which ones I met and which ones I still need to work on. I have been fortunate to be able to meet at least half of my goals every year. However, I started getting curious about why I meet some goals but not others. I identified two major reasons: the first is that external factors are always out of my control. The second is that the goals that I missed do not have a "big why" behind them. For example, I always meet my goal to stay fit because I want to be healthy so I can enjoy my wealth. So whenever I feel like skipping my cardio day to enjoy an ice cream cone instead, I think of my health. Then I jump on that treadmill and throw the ice cream away. The lesson here is that goals will only be met when is a "big why" behind them. If there's no "big why," don't even bother setting those goals.

When faced with challenges, many people resort to alcohol, drugs, or denial. Instead, use exercise or cardio to deal with stress. A person's physical and mental health are interconnected. When you can get your heartbeat up and start to sweat, you sweat out those toxins and stressors. The day will seem much brighter, and the challenges won't seem as bad. Once you work out the stress in your system, then you can calm down and figure out how to resolve the problems at hand. Bear in mind that rational and analytic thinking will help you make sound decisions, while emotional thinking will lead to mistakes and poor decisions.

Take good care of your body because it's the only place you have to live. When I am not feeling well physically, I often use healing affirmations by saying things like, "I am going to let my body heal itself, I'm healing now by getting more rest, this illness is temporary, and I'm already feeling better." When you experience physical illness, refuse to talk about the disease; instead, visualize feeling good and act as if you are in perfect health. Use the positive mindset to help you heal.

Often, the place of greatest discomfort is also where the largest opportunity lies. That's exactly where you need to go to hit the problem head-on so you can grow. When you're thinking about giving up, you're about to have a breakthrough, so keep at it! Sometimes the best time to do something is when you least feel like doing it, and that's when self-discipline saves the day. And those "somethings" are usually composed of small baby steps in the right direction. Remember, small steps are more powerful than big intentions. Great things are not done by impulse but by a series of tiny victories.

Most noises only distract me and drag me down, so I created a system to filter them out! When I need to focus, I turn off my cell phone and work in a place where I won't be disturbed. Having the right setting where you can focus and work is super important. It is also essential to have a good sleep every night. Studies have shown that we need a minimum of 7 hours of deep sleep to recover fully. And guess what the primary source of distraction is? It's your cell phone! So leave your phone in another room where it's hard to reach so you can have a good sleep every night.

Small steps are more powerful than big intentions. Great things are not done by impulse but by a series of tiny victories.

Chapter 29: Relationship with Others

When I was little, my favorite thing to do was to visit my Uncle Peter on the weekends. He was a charmer, had a great sense of humor, and was always fun to be around. Everyone in the neighborhood loved him and would come to hang out with him by his pool every weekend. He was the type of person that other people naturally wanted to be around. He had charisma! From watching Uncle Peter, I learned that the key to charisma was asking questions and listening to others without interrupting, showing interest in others, paying sincere compliments, being cheerful, and raising others' self-esteem. Try to be interested instead of interesting. Everyone likes to talk about themselves, so ask questions and encourage people to open up. That will make you the most popular person in town.

On the opposite end of the spectrum as Uncle Peter is "Ahole." Ahole brags and shows off, constantly changes the subject to focus on himself, lies all the time, and doesn't say hello or make eye contact. Ahole also likes to give unsolicited advice. You might think you know everything, and you might have the best intentions in the world and want to advise your friends and family. Wrong! Just don't do it. It will come across as arrogant and selfish. A good friend of mine, Angle (who retired at the age of 40), told me once that if you want to help your friends, don't give them money or unsolicited advice; instead, ask them constructive questions and recommend books to them. Teach them how to fish and make a living instead of just giving them fish for a day.

Once in a while, I run into an Ahole. Ahole taught me that the best way to answer an annoying person or situation is simply silence. No response is the best and most effective response! Or you can simply walk away. Never try to reason with a person like Ahole because it would just look like two such people arguing from far away. It's a complete waste of your time. When a person like Ahole tries to argue with you and asks you a question, just treat it like a rhetorical question, and answer, not with a word, but with a big smile.

Whenever I meet a new friend for a meal, male or female, I think it's only fair to split the bill. When the check comes, I pay careful attention to what this new person does. If they have no intention of paying and expect me to pick up the check, that is great! That tells me what type of person they are, and it's a cheap lesson to get to know someone.

Never compromise yourself for the sake of friendship. Life is too short to pretend you're someone else. If you have to act and can't be yourself, the friendship isn't real anyway. If a friendship is so fragile that it couldn't even stand a "hard talk" between friends, that's not true friendship, and it's definitely not worth keeping.

Sometimes, others tell me that my success is just due to dumb luck. My response to them is always the same, "Yes, you are right, I am just lucky!" Just put that question to rest. They have no idea what it takes to be in the top 1% in this world, and I don't have the time or desire to explain how hard I have worked to get to where I am today.

As I mentioned earlier, I manage tenants with my commercial real estate business. Sometimes, tenants say to me that landlords have the easiest jobs. They just need to sit there and collect rent, money just comes in, and the landlord doesn't have to work for it. And my response to them? I just smile and agree with them. I am thinking the whole time that I will let them keep thinking that way so I can stay rich and they will stay poor. That sounds cruel, I know, but it is what it is. I have seen a lot of entitled people in my life. Whenever I see them, I can't run away fast enough. Do all you can to avoid those people; they just suck the life right out of you.

Sometimes people I barely know come to me and ask me for financial advice or tips on becoming successful. I recommend books for them to read. I say, "why don't you come back to me once you are done reading these books? Then I would love to give you some pointers." I have probably said this to over 100 people I have met. Guess how many came back? None! Zero! Zilch! Everyone wants to be rich, but no one wants to put in the effort. Instead, they want a shortcut or someone to tell them precisely what to do to get rich. They don't even want to read a book to get smarter first; it's unfortunate.

Being different in this world is often punished by criticism and exclusion from social groups, but it often leads to success. That's why there's a saying, "the path to success is often lonely." The good thing is that you will have a few good friends and books to keep you company.

Deca-millionaires, people with a net worth of 10+ million dollars, all have the same habits. They all have lots of energy because they exercise daily, welcome criticism, and are always honest with themselves and others. They invest in their own businesses and assets, mutual funds or index funds, but not stocks. Their incomes peak at age 45-55, their net worth peaks at age 55-65, and they earn no less than $1000 per hour. They are also secure enough to be alone and enjoy the wonders and wisdom that solitude and quiet bring. The best thinking is often done in solitude. So it's essential to be comfortable being alone and enjoy what solitude brings.

It's important to make an effort to meet people at any social event. I always ask myself, "Do I want to be a winner and go up to someone and say hello, or do I want to be a loser in the corner staring at my phone?" The answer is easy. When meeting someone, show signs of confidence by always be the first to extend your hand for a firm shake, preferably within the first 3 seconds after initial eye contact. Introduce yourself to everyone and maintain constant eye contact when listening. I always try to remember everyone's name by repeating them immediately after introductions and again when I leave the conversation. Show interest in others' business cards and make positive comments about them. A trick for remembering names is associating them with something unique or memorable about the person in question.

In any social event, kill shyness and awkwardness by using the 5-second rule. When I see someone I want to meet, without thinking or hesitation, I immediately go up to them, reach out my hand, make eye contact, and say, "I'm so glad to meet you."

To make myself stand out from the crowd, I need to introduce myself in the order of who/what/why. This is how I introduce myself when I go to a party: "I am Jason. I run and operate affordable housing. When my parents first immigrated to the US, they always had difficulty finding a place to live. So I made it my mission to help new immigrants and the underprivileged find housing for their families." People may not remember my name, but they will always remember my story.

I start every conversation with, "I am just having a wonderful day today, you?" Keep the conversation light. Gossip is like poison; that's why little people love it. So do yourself a favor and stay away from gossip! Also, everyone craves praise, so don't be stingy when saying wonderful things about others.

If you talk more about yourself than others, it is a sign of selfishness. Plus, you don't learn anything when you are talking. So stop showing off and talking about yourself, and instead ask interesting questions and listen. Then you will become the most popular person at any social event.

Everyone is different, and sometimes disagreements happen. Before getting into an argument with someone, ask yourself, "Is this that important?" Most of the time, the answer is no. Big people listen; small people talk. I love saying the phrase, "tell me more." It wins me friends, and I also gain knowledge for myself.

Whenever you leave a conversation, ask yourself, "does that person feel better about themselves?" People crave praise and recognition, so be generous and give it to them. In addition, drop a personal note or phone call after meeting new friends, and they will remember you!

Jason A. Scott

I love saying the phrase, "tell me more." It wins me friends, and I also gain knowledge for myself.

In your personal life, surround yourself with kind people who have integrity. This world is already exhausting enough when you have to deal with people from all walks of life; the last thing you need to do is go home to the same thing. So when meeting new people or making new friends, I always keep those criteria in mind. For example, someone I met not too long ago, Alex, is highly successful and has a great reputation in his field. I met him through a mutual friend. We decided to go hiking together in a group of 4 people. I initially thought it was a short 2-hour hike. It turned out to be a 6-hour strenuous hike over several mountains and on muddy paths. Since this was not what I expected, I wore my regular walking shoes instead of the required hiking shoes. It was a strenuous hike, and I slipped all over the place. Alex saw what was happening, and he was kind enough to help me along the way. He also slowed down his pace on purpose so that I could keep up with the group. This act of kindness really impressed me! You can really get to know a person after spending some time with them, and I appreciated and will always remember his kindness to me that day. It is wonderful that he has achieved so much in his career, but his inner kindness is what earned my respect. We have since become excellent friends, and I am grateful for his friendship. I can see our friendship becoming meaningful and long-lasting.

In business or life, I always try to surround myself with people who are motivated and driven. To give you an example, I recently got reacquainted with a high school friend, Chris, whom I had not seen for a long time. Chris is an expert in commercial real estate, so we often talked about the real estate field. Recently, he brought up a new trend that could potentially turn into a unique business opportunity, and we discussed it over the phone. The very next day, I received an email about some research he had done overnight on the topic. Now that's what a "go-getter" does; I was impressed. When he saw a potential opportunity, he did his homework right away because he knew that time is money and good opportunities don't wait for anyone. Going through life, you will see many people talk about wanting to be successful, but few who take action. Chris is one of those few.

I am ecstatic when I see people around me succeed. I am truly happy for them, especially if they are people I have touched or mentored in the past. For example, Ben is a good friend of mine from my college days. He started his own consulting company about ten years ago after working for a major IT conglomerate. After building up the business and growing the company to over 200 employees, he recently sold it to an IT unicorn for a 20 million dollar payday. The minute I heard the news, I jumped up and down in ecstasy! My dad was with me at the time. He thought I had just won the lottery. But no, I was just so happy for Ben! The way I look at it, a great friend of mine finally succeeded after years of hard work, and he was kind enough to share the news of his success with me. That makes my day! It's like a double dose of happiness for both him and me. Yes, I am a successful person in my own right, but seeing others around me do well in life, especially those I care about, is more thrilling and inspiring to me than anything else in the world.

I like to be with a community that fits well with my values. Surround yourself with honest, smart, straightforward people and avoid judgmental complainers. It's easy to find out if you are around the right people. Keep asking yourself, "when I am with this person, do I get closer or farther away from my ideal self?"

Whenever I get to visit someone in their home, the first thing I do is look through their bookshelves to see what types of books they read. Similarly, whenever I meet someone new, I ask them about their favorite authors or books. You can tell a lot about a person from the books they read. To my surprise, out of every ten people I ask this particular question, only one tells me they read regularly. Five out of ten tell me they can't remember the last time they read a book. No wonder 1% of the population controls 90% of the wealth in this world! The other 99% are too busy living their lives on autopilot instead of reading and making themselves more successful. Just to give you a glimpse of my collection, I have read over 30+ books on building wealth, 20+ books on self-discipline and motivation, and over 40 books on the real estate business. And people still wonder why I am successful in my field. Becoming successful isn't hard; just read!

Jason A. Scott

It's easy to get anything you want in life; however, if you want something, you need to give it first. For example, if you are walking past a stranger on the street and smile first, the other person will smile back at you almost every time. In addition to making someone else smile, you also make yourself feel good. It's a win-win! If you want love, then you have to give love first. Go and hug someone, show people that you care, and it will come back to you tenfold.

Becoming successful isn't hard; just read!

Be respectful of others by not texting or surfing when they are talking. With so much technology and news moving so fast around us, it can be difficult not to check our phones constantly. But if you care about the person you are talking to, show them basic respect by giving them your full attention.

Let's talk some more about using cell phones. I turn my phone off at night, and I try to limit my daily cell phone use to less than three hours. There are several apps for keeping track of daily phone usage if you need help. I have found that less phone usage equals less stress and improves my overall well-being. I also turn off all app notifications, only check my phone once every hour, and never answer unscheduled phone calls. If it's important, they can leave a voice mail.

Treasure every moment when you are with someone you love because you will have less time with them than you think. For example, assuming you and your parents are close and healthy, you might still have another 20 years with them. But when you think about it, 20 years is not that long. What if you only see them once or twice a year? That's a total of 40 times over the next 20 years. That is not much time at all! So treasure every moment you spend with loved ones because it may be the last.

If you want something, you need to give it first.

During any conversation, I ask questions, show interest, smile, offer caring gestures, point out the positives, and encourage whomever I meet. It might seem like nothing to me, but it will affect others significantly in positive ways. I might have even made someone's day or changed their lives. Try not to talk about yourself and keep a low profile. Instead, be energic and positive all the time when you are around people. It is infectious; everyone wants to be around someone cheerful!

Ever since I was a little boy, I've liked to use exaggerated facial expressions, such as sticking out my tongue when taking a selfie. And why not? I'm an interesting person and have a big personality, and an unexpected expression is fun!

Be sociable and open yourself up to the world. Become addicted to meeting new people. You can meet people anywhere! I find it easy to meet new people at the gym. You can simply say, "Need some water, hi, my name is Jason," "Need a spot?", "Nice shoes." Another comfortable place to meet people is in book stores or while I am traveling. The key is to build a connection first with a genuine compliment or a comment about what they are doing or wearing and get a smile or "yes" in return. Then you can talk about whatever you want to build that comfortable feeling.

It is better to have few friends with deep connections than many superficial acquaintances in your personal life. The opposite is true in business. My dad taught me that it's better to have just 4 to 5 close friends who would pick up your call in the middle of the night than 50 superficial friends who don't care if you live or die. In business, you will want an extensive network of superficial acquaintances. Remember, never go into business with close friends or family!

Never offer advice if not asked, and don't ever try to be a savior. People will do whatever they want to do. Furthermore, if they did not ask for your advice, stay out of their lives. Spend less time fixating on everyone else and instead spend more time focusing on your own wellness.

Sometimes during a conversation, someone tries to tell me a story that I have heard before. Even if I have heard the story before, I will pretend that

I'm hearing it for the first time. I try to live it as a new experience every time. Realize that everyone likes to tell their stories, especially older folks. Instead of saying that they have told that story before, keep your mouth shut and let them enjoy telling it again. This way, they will enjoy themselves, while you get to enjoy helping them to be happy. Now that's a win-win.

When you are complimented, try to be gracious and thank everyone around you for their support along the way. Then, share the success with them, so they also get a double dose of happiness. My Daily Five is where I pay compliments to or thank at least five different strangers a day. It sounds like an effortless gesture, but it will tremendously brighten their days and, in turn, make me happy when I see smiles on their faces. What you give, you shall receive back tenfold.

A friendship can last a season or a lifetime. Always keep an eye out for lasting friendships when you meet new people. They are tough to find, but don't give up! Lasting friendships are out there just waiting to be made.

Chapter 30: Dating

Everyone deserves to be loved. If you are lucky, you might just find the love of your life during your lifetime. To do that, you will need to start dating so you can get to know people and vice versa. I have dated quite a bit during my adulthood, and I would like to share what I have learned. You may disagree with some of my conclusions, but I am simply sharing my experiences.

If you are single and see an attractive person, use the 5-Second Rule. Just walk up to them and start talking. You can talk about anything or simply say hello. If you wait longer than 5 seconds, your brain will likely try to talk you out of it. So if you see someone you like, just go up and say hi! What is the worst that can happen? They don't say hi back? You feel embarrassed? Big deal! Do the same thing at any social event. Be bold and seek out the things you want in life.

When I start dating someone, I try to let them use their imagination. I try to stay a mystery for as long as possible, which makes me more attractive in their eyes. I let them have competition anxiety and give hints of implied non-exclusivity. I communicate mysteriously with my behavior so that they can draw their own conclusions. Be confident; no one wants to date someone with low self-esteem.

Leave the phone at home when going on a date with a loved one. They deserve all of your attention. Shower them with quality time; just listening is one of the most thoughtful gifts you can give. I also like to do new things together, like volunteering and meditation.

When I love someone, and my heart tells me that I want to be with them, I always keep in mind that my happiness is not dependent on anything external or anyone else's approval. The only opinion you should care about is your own.

Neediness is not sexy, but detachment is super sexy. Dating is like juggling; you want to have as many balls, or options, in the air as possible. When the other person senses that you have plenty of options, you instantly become more attractive. It's human nature to want to have things you cannot have. So make yourself scarce or present a perception of scarcity.

When it comes to dating, I am a late bloomer. I did not start dating until I was in college. There was this one time I was dating a girl I liked, and things were going so well. Then suddenly, she just stopped taking my calls and would disappear for days. It was the first time I ever dealt with a relationship challenge, so I was a total wreck. I wouldn't eat or sleep for days, and I just stayed in my apartments all day and didn't even go to class. Brian, my roommate at the time, came to me and asked me what was wrong. I told him that my girlfriend still told me she loved me but took days to return my calls, so I didn't know what to do. Brian said something to me then that I will never forget. He said, "Do not listen to what she says; look at what she does. Actions don't lie. Obviously, she's dating someone else now, and you don't believe it because you are in love and aren't thinking straight. This girl is just messing with your mind man, just get over her and move on." I realized he was right. I stopped calling her and started seeing other people right away. I got over her within a short time, all thanks to Brian. As a side note, Brian and I became best of friends along with my other roommate. For the past 20 years, we have always been there for each other, and I appreciate him.

Do not listen to what she says; look at what she does. Actions don't lie.

When I am in a relationship, I split expenses based on what each of us earns at the time. Unfortunately, some girls expect the guys to pick up the check at restaurants. Those girls are the ones I am not interested in dating. You can tell a lot about a person when you see how they save or spend their money. People's character shows through their actions, so if a girl orders lobster on a first date and expects you to pay, you know you are dating a gold digger.

I don't recommend that anyone gets married unless they want to have children. If you decide you want to get married, please do two things asap. First, have a financial discussion with your partner to make sure you are on the same wavelength regarding personal finance. Second, have them sign a prenup asap. Asking them to sign a prenup does two things: it tests them to see if they are marrying you for your money, and most importantly, it allows you to see their worst side before the wedding. Never apologize for asking them to sign a prenup. If they are genuinely a good person, they should be happy to sign it. It is not heartless to ask for a prenup; it's common sense.

It is not heartless to ask for a prenup; it's common sense.

Chapter 31: Managing People

As the owner of my own business, I know that hiring the right staff and managing them well are the most challenging tasks a manager has to do. When dealing with existing colleagues, you will get first-class results if you treat them all like first-class people. When hiring a new employee, I realize that employees tend to stay longer when they consider their work to be meaningful. What does an employee view as meaningful work? It's a job with complexity, autonomy, and where there's a relationship between effort & reward. Try to give them those three things, and you will do well.

With any business, it's better to have a system or protocol in place so employees know how to handle all sorts of situations. This way, you don't have to be in the office all the time to make decisions. Since the writing is on the wall, everyone knows how to do their job and deal with all sorts of events. Of course, everyone must be crystal clear on the protocols and execute the protocols 100% of the time.

I always try to have office meetings standing up and encourage people to speak as quickly and efficiently as possible. The focus of the meeting should be "What's the next action step?" Try to provide clarity and focus. During the meeting, stay quiet and let others talk. Don't show strong facial expressions so no one can tell if you agree with them or not. Always be the last one to speak after hearing what everyone else has to say.

Whenever a subordinate comes to you with a problem, ask the following three questions:

1) What's on your mind?

2) What else?

3) How can I help?

Those questions ensure that you have all the information to answer their questions. Also, don't rush to answer their question if you aren't sure or need more time to consider. If you don't have the answers for them right away, simply tell them that you need to think about it and get back to them. Time is your friend; use the time to think things through. Most of the time, thinking through a problem will help you develop a better solution or answer.

When an employee comes to me about some difficulty, I don't offer a solution, even if I have one. Instead, I ask questions so they can come up with their own solution. I ask questions like, "How do you see this?" "How do you plan to resolve this?" or "How do we follow up?" This way, I train them to think independently instead of coming to me every time they have a problem.

As the boss, I always try to be positive, pay recognition, praise good practice, appreciate efforts, encourage progress, and celebrate success as often as I can. People change by feeling good, not feeling bad.

I often ask my employees for feedback: "How would you rate me as a manager on a scale of 1 to 10?" "What would it take to make it a 10?" Then I thank them for caring enough to share their opinions with me.

Honesty and straightforwardness is the best policy. When talking to my staff, I try to listen carefully with direct eye contact, watch their body language, ask for clarification, and always watch for an unspoken message. I only speak the truth because I know it'll come back to bite me later on if I don't.

When I see employees who might be having a problem, I say, "I can't help but notice you don't look like you're in a really good space. I'm concerned.

What's wrong?" or "You don't look happy. What's going on? Please tell me because I can't fix what I don't know."

Whenever I am dealing with an office issue that brings up strong emotions, I always keep my composure and don't show any emotions in front of my staff. Employees should only see their leader as calm and collected. I also know bad decisions are usually made when strong emotions are involved. In these situations, I opt to "sleep on it." Most of the time, I come up with a way better solution when I wake up the following morning. Give yourself time to think things through.

People change by feeling good, not feeling bad.

How should you behave in the workplace? I keep the following list of actions taped to my office desk: be a good person, ask how others feel and listen to their responses, give sincere compliments, recognize effort, choose calm and patience, show gratitude, and make others feel good.

When building my team, I only want to hire people that I like. Even if someone is the smartest person in the room and will bring me tons of business, I won't hire them if I don't think we'll get along. Chemistry is that important. You should look forward to going to work on Monday mornings because of the people you work with. I also believe in a couple of sayings you might have heard before: "Get the right people on the bus into the right seats, and get the wrong people off the bus." Also, "Hire slowly and fire quickly." I mentioned the second one in one of the previous chapters in the book. I follow these two principles to a T when hiring new staff. I also find that it might take me 3-4 firings before filling one open position. Good help is hard to find, and every business is about people, so if you find the right person for a job, overpay them by 10-20% of the market price. Give them every reason to stay!

A busy CEO is a bad CEO. If they are busy all the time, that means they either do not have the right staff or do not delegate well. They could also simply not be a good leader or know what they are doing. It's imperative to find the right help, and it's often said that one good employee beats 50 bad or lazy ones. Instead of working on day-to-day operations, a good CEO should spend all their time finding the right employees or doing critical thinking to set forth a plan for the company's future.

If an employee needs improvement in a particular area, I say to them, "Jesse, if I see ways in which you can improve your performance, what would you like me to do?" The response will always be that they want me to let them know. But now their response to my suggestions will be much better because they've permitted me to offer advice and feedback. For example, in the case where an employee just finished a job and is asking me what I think, instead of telling her what I think right away, I would say, "well, how do you think you did?" This way, I know what she is thinking first before I even respond."

Always use positive reinforcement with your employees. For example, I walk around the office and try to catch them doing good things, and I compliment them right away when they are. Everyone craves attention and compliments. So when I compliment them and even celebrate with them when they are doing the right things, the behavior will continue. If you celebrate often and immediately, it's effective. It lets them feel good about themselves and wanting to do a good job. So find ways to celebrate even the smallest things!

Whenever I implement a new protocol, instead of just asking my employees to do it, I first ask for their advice. In figuring out what to do, I lead them to the very solution I have in mind so that they think it was their idea. This way, they will be excited to execute the new protocol. People don't like to be told what to do, but they love being told that their ideas are brilliant.

Chapter 32: Communication & The Art of Selling

I don't care who you are or what industry you're in, if you want to do well financially in the world we live in today, you must be able to sell. It does not matter if it's a product, a service, or your personality. If you can't sell or don't want to, it will be very difficult for you to make it in this world. When I hear people saying they are not good with people and would rather do administrative jobs, I feel sad for them. What a load of cr*p! Most successful people are great salespeople. You either become good at selling or get used to being poor for the rest of your life. Yes, you might be a shy person, but you can learn how to sell and better your life. Be a winner and learn how to sell!

The following are some tips I learned on selling.

Buyers usually go through 7 stages of emotions when making a purchase: 1) the buyer is excited, 2) the buyer focuses on the negative, 3) the buyer fears they might be overpaying, 4) the buyer is regretting not buying the product, 5) the buyer accepts that they should just buy the product, 6) the buyer feels happiness after making the purchase, and 7) the buyer feels relieved that the whole thing is over and that they finally got what they wanted. Knowing which emotional steps your buyer is in will determine how you can best facilitate a potential sale.

Don't try to "sell" a product or service; instead, act as a consultant for the customer using the following phrases: "we've all been there," "I sympathize with what you are going through," "I understand it's a hard decision, but it'll get easier, and we'll deal with it together."

If you offer a high-end product such as a luxury home that has a long sales cycle, the worst that can happen is what's called a standstill. A standstill is when a buyer and seller are too far apart on price, and no one wants to budge. What you need to do is encourage either party to make an offer or counteroffer, remind your client of the sunken cost of time and money, or ask the two parties to split the difference. The key is to keep the dialog going and close the deal while it's still hot.

Use the following simple communication rules when conversing with others: smile, listen without interrupting, listen more and talk less, give sincere appreciation, compliment others, and be modest. It's also my rule to always wait three seconds before responding to others, as it gives me time to think and be sure they're finished talking. When I interrupt others by accident, I say, "I am sorry, please continue."

When communicating with others, keep in mind that most people operate on the "feeling level," so when someone seems upset while they're talking, answer their question by asking, "how does that make you feel?"

Everyone craves encouragement and recognition, so give it to them. It's free, and it makes them feel good about themselves. You are bringing happiness to their world, so why not? Just do it! Be intentional in looking for ways to compliment others. Don't be stingy using words like "thank you" and "please." "Thank you" always comes with a smile, and "please" gets results. When a barber tells his customer that "any hairstyle would look good on you," his tips increase by 35 percent!

If you are selling an expensive product or service, the correct method is to show your client a product in their price range and then wow them with the same product in the high-end range. For example, if you are selling someone a car, you would first show them a car in their price range of 20 thousand dollars, then show them vehicles in the price range of 40 thousand dollars to create that "wow moment." Close the deal by having them settle on a car with a price tag somewhere in the middle.

Every product has a story. Find it, and the product will sell, even with something as simple as a bakery. The story could be about the founder who started the business, for example, or something unique about the ingredients you use. Be creative! Take the time to come up with a story that you can tell your customers. Remember that people might not remember your name, but they will never forget your story if you make it interesting.

One of the most interesting psychology concepts is the "framing of the mind." This concept comes in handy when trying to sell a product to someone. Studies have shown that people will confirm whatever they focus on. Ask potential customers questions like "are you dissatisfied with their service?" "Are you unhappy?" These questions frame your customers as being unhappy with their existing product or service. Now they will be ready for your pitch! It is also much easier to influence someone's decision by getting them to focus on something than by trying to change their attitude directly.

You have seen people on the street going around asking others to do surveys so that they can sell you a product or service while you do the survey. When they use the opener "do you consider yourself a helpful person?" and then ask to do the survey, the success rate goes from 29% to 75%. Think about how powerful framing of the mind is when trying to get people to agree to something.

People tend to reciprocate. For example, when Costco offers samples to their customers, it results in 40% more sales. During negotiation, take it a step further, offer something, and immediately ask for something in return.

Chapter 33: Investing

I am a real estate investor, and I know a thing or two about investing in apartments, but I have relatively limited knowledge about investing in the stock market. Even with my limited knowledge of stock investing, I have been doing it for the past 10+ years and have done quite well, so I would like to share what I have learned. Stocks are unpredictable, so you have to be ready to lose all or most of your money before you start investing. Before you take the plunge, make sure this is something you can stomach.

Act now on opportunities that make sense. The only thing Warren Buffet has hanging up on his office wall is a "Ted Williams Hitting Map." It's a map that shows the percentage of Ted Williams (one of the greatest hitters in the history of baseball) swings that resulted in a hit. It turns out that when Ted swings at a pitch that's in the middle of the hitting zone, more than 80% of the time, it results in a hit. The moral is that you don't need to swing at all the pitches to do well, only those in the dead middle. Patience is a virtue, especially in the stock market.

I first invested in the US stock market when I was still in college. I bought Yahoo stock during the internet boom in the early 2000s at $98 with borrowed money, and I lost pretty much all of it when I was forced to sell my shares at $12 due to margin calls. I was devasted, and I vowed to learn everything I could about the stock market so something like that wouldn't happen to me again. I carefully observed the stock market during the Internet bust, the Solomon crisis, the housing crisis, and Covid pandemic crisis. The following is what I have learned. Everyone knows to buy low and sell high. Warren Buffet says you want to be greedy when others are fearful and fearful when others are greedy. But that is easier said than done! Imagine the Dow Jones drops 500 points in one day (which has happened); anyone would be fearful. Many wealthy people, even some of the top 1%, sold all their stock holdings during March 2020 when Covid started. It's just human nature; you can't help but be afraid. I have learned that a significant part of the stock market is basic human psychology. When people are scared, stocks will tank.

One of the most interesting things about investing is that human emotions drive the market: the fear of losing money and the desire to make money. You simply have to decide where the market is in the economic cycle, and then you can make a fortune. The economic cycle generally lasts 8-11 years.

There are only two laws in the stock market. Number one, the stock market will always go up when you drag out the time horizon. Number two, only investors with self-discipline will make money in the stock market. For the past several years, I have slowly gotten back into the market. I came up with a formula that I want to share with you. I call it my Cost Average Monthly Investing Method. Thanks to this formula, I have averaged about 10-12% return over the past four years. Once again, I am not a stockbroker, nor do I have the license to advise people on buying stocks, but this is what I do.

I split up the money I want to invest in the market into two piles, putting half in pile "Money A" and half in pile "Money B."

1) With the Money A funds, I invest 80% in an S&P index fund and 20% in a bond fund.

2) With the Money B funds or my monthly investment, I use the cost average method to invest. Every month I invest a fixed amount of money into the market with the same ratio, 80% into an index fund and 20% into a bond fund. I set up auto-investing online, where my online brokerage automatically invests according to those ratios, so I don't even have to look at how the market is doing.

3) If the market drops by 30%, the alert I set up informs me via email, and then I sell all my bond shares and split that money into three even

piles. I invest the first pile into the index fund, then invest the second pile when the market drops another 10%, and invest the last third pile when the market drops yet another 10%.

By this time, the stock market has dropped 50% from its all-time high, and the chances of it going any lower are slim. Even if it does go lower, I just stick to my guns and ride it out. One requirement for this type of investing is that you have a stable income and don't need to sell stocks to feed your family. This formula makes sense, and it's easy to follow, especially for me. I am the type of person who hates to look at the stock market and worry about losing or making money. Since everything is set up to invest automatically, I don't have to do anything.

The hardest part of investing is to have the self-discipline not to buy individual stocks, which is both very risky and very tempting. Also, do not be fearful when everyone around you is scared. However, speaking from personal experience, I think the chances of making money with this particular method of investing are pretty high.

Most people invest in the stock market to get ready for retirement. And everyone has heard of the four percent rule, which means, on average, the stock market will go up around four percent annually. I am a bit more conservative; I only expect a two percent annual increase from investing in the market when I eventually retire. That's a way safer bet.

With my real estate investments, I often have to ask banks for loans to buy assets. One of my observations when dealing with banks over the years is that the best time to ask them for money is when I need it the least. How ironic! The bank usually goes through an "underwriting" process before they grant a loan. This is where they review my financials, including income and credit, to see what kind of risk I have to repay the loan. A person's financial record is often a reflection of a pattern of behavior and choices a person makes. In my case, I have a high credit score, impeccable credit history, and a decent income, so the interest rates a bank will offer me will be low since I am in the low-risk category. My risk will be lowest when I don't need any money, so this is also when I will get the best offers from banks. That's why I like to refinance my properties whenever I can, so I can pull cash out of my assets with low-interest rates and be ready for my next investment opportunity. This concept is very similar to the job market. The best time to look for a new job is when you just started a new job; it's a different situation, but the concept is the same.

The other virtue necessary to make it to the top is patience, which might be the most difficult to put into practice. Take investing in the stock market, for example. If everyone knows you want to buy low and sell high, then why do 99% of investors do the opposite? It's because when the market goes up, it takes tremendous self-discipline to just sit on the sidelines and not do anything while everyone else makes bank thanks to the rising stock prices. It also takes immense courage to buy stock during a recession when people lose their jobs, and the future looks so gloomy. Investing is not easy. Only those with self-discipline can be successful, and they are that 1%.

The famous investor George Soros said something that resonated with me. He said, "Good investing is boring. If you are having fun, you are probably losing money. Buying & Holding is the only real investing." I believe this principle holds for every type of investor, including real estate. My good friend Mike is one of the few people I know who live by this principle when investing. He will spend years sitting on the sidelines in the biggest bull market, but as soon as stocks tank by 30-40%, without batting an eye, he puts all his money into the stock market and just waits for it to rebound. He's one of the most successful investors I know, and he only trades once every ten years! Minimum effort with maximum results. That's what I call intelligent investing.

Good investing is boring. If you are having fun, you are probably losing money. Buying & Holding is the only real investing.

The famous Charles Munger also said something that resonated with me. He said, "Big money is not in the buying and selling of stocks. It's in the waiting. Success in stocks means being very patient but aggressive when it's time." Very few actions are required to earn massive rewards, so choose and act wisely.

Big money is not in the buying and selling of stocks. It's in the waiting.

The above is what I have learned from investing in the stock market with my own money. I am not a market adviser, so please consult with financial advisors before investing your own money. Invest wisely, and good luck!

Chapter 34: Commercial Real Estate

It is not easy to make money straight out of college. As a recent college graduate, you will be at least $100,000 in debt. In addition, there is inflation of 5% per year to take into account, the interest you have to pay on your student loans, insurance for your health/car/home, taxes on your income, taxes on everything you buy, and taxes on your property if you are lucky enough to own a home. The odds are stacked against you before you even find your first job.

Looking at the list of expenses above, it seems impossible to succeed in this world, so how do rich people do it? The key is to minimize as many of those expenses as possible. So how do you go about doing that? Well, in a nutshell, you can 1) structure your assets and income properly to delay paying taxes for as long as possible, 2) hedge inflation with assets, and 3) use real estate depreciation to shelter your income.

Out of all the investment tools, I have found commercial real estate to be the best one. If done correctly, it can be the most rewarding and reliable source of income. After all, everyone needs a place to live. Of course, I am a little biased since commercial real estate is how I made my money. My only regret is that I should have started to invest in real estate sooner. But as they always say, better late than never.

I, like many other people, am averse to debt. I was always taught that you shouldn't be buying anything if you don't have enough money. When I first started buying real estate, I had a very negative view of borrowing money to purchase assets. That all changed when I met my real estate broker Doug. Doug has over 40 years of experience in the field of commercial real estate, and I have learned so much from him these past five years! He is a man of the highest integrity, and I would not purchase a single piece of property without him acting as my agent. The first thing he taught me is that debt is my friend. There is no way to make any money if I don't borrow money from the bank and leverage it. If done correctly, that means borrowing the right amount under the correct terms. Debt will expedite my path to financial freedom if done correctly.

Many books have been written on investing in commercial real estate, so I will not go into too much detail. However, I will briefly touch upon some of the important principles I have learned about borrowing money to invest in real estate.

1) Find the longest mortgage amortization schedule, preferably 30 years fixed rate, with the lowest annual loan constant. This will help you to maximize your monthly cash flow. Remember, cash is king. Profit is made from debt, not asset appreciation. So make sure it's a well-structured loan.

2) Inflation is good for you since you can just keep raising the rent. However, always think of inflation in terms of reduced purchase power. You never want to hold on to cash; instead, buy assets, which will generate income for you.

3) Pay as little down payment/fees as possible. Your goal is to reduce the actual money you have to pay now. Instead, try to pay with the future nominal dollar, which is worthless after inflation.

4) Delay paying off the loan as far into the future as possible since money will be worthless in the future after inflation.

5) I love business networking events, but remember, business and emotion don't mix well. If you mix business and emotions, you have a big problem. In my years of experience dealing with my tenants, even

though many of them are friendly people, I never get too close or become their friends. I fully understand that renting to them is my business. This is where I make a living. It's not a place to make friends, sympathize with their problems, or empathize with why they cannot pay rent on time. It's essential to draw a red line between your business and your personal life!

6) When looking for a new tenant, I prefer to rent to people with stable incomes. Some people live on a fixed income, and that's OK. However, they are looking to cut expenses and spend the rest of their lives in the same place. For me, this means there will be less turnover, and less turnover means more profits for me in the long run.

Suppose you are interested in going into commercial real estate. There are many books on the subject. You can also read a book I wrote on this topic titled "Millionaire Landlord Secrets." It's available online on Amazon.

Chapter 35: Goal Setting & Visualization

I, like most people, make New Year's resolutions. I list my goals for the coming year on January 1st. Unfortunately, most people don't meet their goals or get anywhere close to them, while I usually achieve 60% of my goals. I want to share with you how I make that possible.

My list of goals is very detailed, and every plan has a realistic deadline. I write up a list of goals and all the action steps required to meet those goals. Then I tape that list onto my bathroom mirror. When I brush my teeth every morning, I stare at that list and go over it in my mind. Doing this gives me a daily reminder of what my goals are. I want to make sure that whatever I am working on that day is helping me achieve those goals.

I also announce my goals to the world by telling my friends and everyone I know. For some magical reason, the world helps me achieve my goals every time! I am not religious, but things like this happen to me time after time. Once I have set clear goals and announce them to the world, it seems like everything and everyone around me wants to help me achieve them.

Ever since I was little, I always knew I would be rich; I never doubted it for a minute. One of the things on my morning ritual board is how much net worth I will have by the end of the year. I have not missed this particular goal for the past six years! I read my goals daily, sometimes even 20 times or more. The power of repeatedly seeing the end goad is so strong that it becomes real.

There is no option but to achieve your goals, so your brain will subconsciously find a way to achieve the desired result.

Chapter 36: Negotiation

With any type of business, you will be making deals with customers, vendors, and contractors. Since you are dealing with people and money, you must have good negotiation skills. I have learned some excellent negotiation tactics over the years that I would like to share with you now. Please note, some of the strategies listed below might seem manipulative at first glance, but they are not. Both parties want to get the best out of the negotiations, and the worst that can happen is that both parties leave without making a deal. If negotiation is done correctly, you can and will achieve a win-win where both parties are happy with the end result.

Warren Buffet said, "Never buy retail." You can negotiate everything everywhere. It doesn't matter if you are in a department store or a street stand. Just say, "is that the best you can do?" What's the worst that can happen? They might say no, but they won't throw you out of the store or anything. Simply uttering those words probably takes three seconds of your time. You can get potentially get a great deal and save some money, so why not? It might be the fastest money you'll ever make!

Always ask for more than you want. Usually, you will get more than you want because the other party will almost always want to split the difference down the middle. So always low ball on the first counter, but express flexibility. Bracket strategy is when there's a bracket between the seller's high asking price and the buyer's low offering price. 90% of the time, the strike price will be somewhere in the middle. Your best strategy is always to get the other party to make the first offer, so you will be in a better position to set the bracket.

Never buy retail. You can negotiate everything everywhere.

Suppose you are in a face-to-face negotiation, and the other party makes the first offer. In that case, your immediate reaction should be to cringe no matter what the offer is. This communicates that their price is outrageous, and they need to give you a better price to seal the deal.

Always make an offer with a specific dollar amount. Let's say you are making an offer on an item. You need to make the offer amount as specific as possible. For example, using a specific number such as $115,050 is better than $115,000 because it gives the other party the impression that you have done your homework. There's a legitimate reason behind that exact number.

Never argue with your counterpart; instead, respond using the FFF strategy: "I understand exactly how you FEEL, many have FELT the same way, but with a closer look, they FOUND that..." Avoid being contentious. Use the word "feel" as much as possible when asking questions: "And how do you feel about that?"

Be a reluctant Seller. "I don't know. This antique has been in the family for a very long time, and I am not sure if my wife will let me sell this piece of art...."

Always decide on your "walk-away" point before starting a negotiation. Your walk-away point is the highest price you are willing to pay for the product in question. Don't overpay in the heat of the moment! That's why buying in a live auction is such a bad idea. Most people end up paying more than they intended to!

Use the higher authority gambit. Never tell the other party that you are the final decision maker. Even if the other party knows you are the CEO of the company, say, "well, I will need to check with my board of directors."

If there are many terms to be negotiated, resolve minor issues first to build momentum. Always give significant concessions on the minor issues and then smaller concessions toward the end when dealing with the bigger issues. Always ask for a trade-off when giving up something, and ask for it immediately. Always make a big deal of what you are giving up.

Be aware that 80% of concessions are given during the last 20 mins of negotiation, so tie up details early. However, the longer the other party spends in negotiations, the more sunken costs they've accumulated, and the more flexible they become.

Even if you know you have won at the end of the negotiation, never, ever gloat. Instead, always let the other party walk away thinking they have won. "Wow, I have to admit you are a great negotiator, but I appreciate that you are a straight shooter, and you did this with integrity from start to finish. Great job."

It might be smart to sometimes act dumb during a negotiation, "I don't know, what do you think?" Savvy negotiators let others do all the talking so that they can do most of the thinking.

Ask as many questions as possible, even if the other party doesn't answer. Most people are not good actors, and their answers are usually written on their faces. I have learned a lot from reading others' facial expressions. Don't give up just because the other party says "no." Realize that "no" is simply an opening to negotiation. It's a stepping stone on the way to "yes."

In most negotiations, whoever speaks first loses, so practice being comfortable in awkward silence. Let the other party talk first.

Chapter 37: Art of Asking for More

Never settle for anything mediocre. When you go on vacation, always ask for a courtesy upgrade. First, ask the airline ground crew at the airport check-in counter if the flight is full; if not, ask for an upgrade to first class. At hotels, ask for a free courtesy upgrade to a bigger room with a view. At the ticketing counter of a show, ask for better seats if the theatre is not at max capacity. When I ask for these upgrades, I get them around 99% of the time! All you have to do is ask; it is that easy. Then, grow a thick skin and ask for more! Just dress professionally and be nice.

Practice asking for more everywhere you go and with everything you do. It's just a numbers game. Be numb to rejections.

AAA is one of my favorite acronyms. No, I am not talking about triple-A car club; instead, it is an acronym for "Ask Ask Ask." You are never going to get something if you don't ask for it. No one is going to help you unless you first ask for their help. Never assume that someone else knows what you are thinking. If you need someone's assistance, ask for it. They can either say yes or no; either way, you know exactly where they stand and can deal with it accordingly. Studies have shown that most people are happy to help a stranger when they ask for assistance. Wouldn't you?

Grow a thick skin and ask for more!

Everywhere I go, I expect the best because I deserve the best, and I start by asking for it. My principle is that if I ask, then I shall receive. So the more I ask, the more I will receive. If I ask and get rejected, so what? I am back to where I started and don't lose anything. So I encourage everyone to ask away.

Asking for more is especially important in business. Before I go into a meeting to ask my customers for an order, I always visualized them placing the order at the end of the meeting. This way, I act and behave confidently during the meeting as if they have already agreed to place the order. Most of the time, I get that order as expected. So start everything with the assumption that you will get what you ask for. This is a perfect example of using visualization to achieve success!

One of the techniques I use most is called the "Non-response" technique. I have found it to be handy, and you can apply it in almost any situation. I used this fantastic technique once at an airport. I was checking into my flight at the American Airlines counter one day and was told that the flight was overbooked and that I would have to take the next flight. This would make me miss a scheduled appointment. I was not going to let that happen, so I used my "non-response" negotiation technique. I asked the person behind the counter, "what needs to happen for me to be on this plane?" and then didn't say another word. Whatever excuses he gave me, I just remained silent. Eventually, he talked himself into putting me on the plane. Simply state your request and don't speak or move until it is fulfilled.

I was always told when I was a child that "if you have nothing nice to say, you shouldn't say anything at all." That holds true to this day. Just because someone asks you a question does not mean you have to respond. You can treat it as a rhetorical question and remain silent. It's not rude when you choose not to reply, and it's ok to have a silent and awkward moment in any conversation. In business negotiations, silence is golden. Always use it to your advantage. For example, once I was negotiating with one of my vendors, and I had him make the first offer as I always do. Then I just squinted my eyes to make it seem like his price was too high, and I continued to sit there and not say a word. After 30 seconds of silence, he dropped his price without me saying a word. Silence is truly golden, and it can even make you money!

When it comes to love, don't take things for granted. Ask for hugs, ask for love. Every human being needs 12 hugs a day, so ask away. And when you are attracted to someone, go up to them and ask for their phone number. It might be a start of a beautiful relationship, and it will never happen if you don't bother asking in the first place.

Sometimes, keeping your mouth shut is the best idea. You can only learn new things when you let others speak. You will certainly not learn anything new while you are talking. So keep quiet, and maybe, just maybe, you will learn something of great value! The rich are usually people of few words, but when they speak, people listen.

Chapter 38: Living with Purpose

Everyone needs to live with a purpose. Without one, you are just walking through life in your sleep. However, not everyone has the same purpose. Therefore, it will be well worth it for you to sit down and think about the big "why."

For me, my purpose is to experience this wonderful world and serve others. I am a total believer in thinking positively and acting kindly. Be kind to others all the time, especially when others are less fortunate than you. There are many simple gestures of kindness: opening the door for a stranger, paying for the next guy's coffee at the Starbucks drive-through, or simply saying thank you and hello, or paying someone a genuine compliment. You can do a small act of kindness anywhere and at any moment to brighten someone else's day, and magically, your act of kindness will radiate outward to the world around you.

Look for kindness and appreciation in every situation. See this world in an abundance of air, water, sun, and love. When I think abundance and only focus on what I already have, magically, the right people appear, and the right breaks come along.

How you view others is how you view yourself; how you see the world is also how you see yourself. So think of everyone as kind and of the world around you as beautiful.

It is ok to set expectations of yourself, but it's absurd to set expectations of others. Who are you to expect someone else to do something? Everyone has their own agenda, and everyone is in a different situation. You have no right, nor do you have the power to make an assumption about someone else or try to change them. Better to focus only on what you can do. After all, you are the successful 1% and have achieved success because you listen to your inner self and instincts.

Look for kindness and appreciation in every situation.

I do things because I want to, and I never expect anything in return. For example, when family and friends want to borrow money from me, I either say no or give them the money without the expectation of getting it back. It's ridiculous to lose a deep connection with someone I love over money. I also do things for others without the expectation of reciprocation; that's the only way to give and serve others.

Live with gratitude. Life is short, and everything and every person in your life is there for a reason, so feel nothing but gratitude toward them. I believe character is defined by what you do when others are not looking. A person's strength is not determined by how much money they have or how strong they are. It's defined by how they treat others in need.

Always be honest, always always always, because the inner peace that results from being honest will create even more happiness. Helping others will help you gain a deep sense of connection and joy. Spend your time and money on beautiful memories, loved ones, and things you love and appreciate. The energy you put into the world, your beliefs, words, and attitudes, is the energy that will come back to you.

Character is defined by what you do when others are not looking.

Chapter 39: Money & Simple Living

Money does not buy happiness, but money does buy freedom, the freedom to do what you want, when you want, with whomever you want, and as much as you want.

Your feelings about money determine your wealth. In this chapter, I will discuss how I view money. Money is not the end goal; it is just a tool to get where I want to be. Money cannot buy happiness once my basic needs are fulfilled, but money can buy freedom. Instead of working every day, I can wake up in the morning and decide what I want to do.

Either positive or negative energy is created when you hold money in your hand, and the type of energy is determined by your attitude. I am always grateful when money is flowing through me. I say thank you when I receive or give away money. Through me, all money becomes "happy money" because I give it positive energy.

How a person views and talks about money will determine how much money they will have. Poor people like to blame others for their lack of fortune; middle-class people talk about things that 'happen to them'; wealthy people talk about new ideas for making money. Choose your conversation topics wisely.

There are two main motivations in the world: love and fear. In almost all cases, we spend money on one or the other. Try to spend money on "love" because you will be creating *happy money*. I like to spend money on unique experiences, and it is never wasted because I made the conscious decision on how I wanted to spend it. Either use money or let money use you.

When you live a healthy lifestyle, you attract money no matter what you do. Even with wealth, it's best to be happy with less. A happy life is not necessarily filled with luxurious material things. A truly happy life is one in which you interact only with people you care about, in places you love, doing what you love. Truly wealthy people are not money rich; they have deep relationships with the ones they love.

Always try to give something extra. Always over tip at a restaurant. The more money you share, the more your money will grow. When you buy material things, always buy quality, not quantity. The goal is to pay twice as much and buy half as many.

Truly wealthy people are not money rich; they have deep relationships with the ones they love.

I have accumulated most of my wealth unconventionally, and now I would like to do the same with my time. Prioritize how you use your time and money and only do things that matter most to you.

My money's job is to make more money, and my job is to live every minute of my life to the fullest. So if I can give money away, that's when I know I control my money, not the other way around.

Everyone has a choice. You can choose a secure job that pays you a fixed salary and where you get to go back to your family at 5 pm every day. Or you can choose to risk it all and start your own company, where you could work 20 hours a day without any guarantee that you will be successful in the end. Of course, a bigger risk will come with more significant rewards.

I still work, not because I have to, but because I want to have a more prosperous and full life. The key is to have minimum financial obligations by keeping expenses low. I can easily live on 2500 dollars a month or 30,000 dollars a year. My overall expenses are low because most of the things I treasure are free: reading, exercising, meditation, traveling, attending musical concerts, practicing self-discipline, and keeping a few strong friendships. Simple things that make you happy are usually free. It's strange; the more money I make, the less money I spend; talk about irony!

The fewer material things you have, the fewer things you have to worry about. If you drive around a beat-up Nissan Altima instead of a fancy Mercedes Benz, you won't have to worry about someone scratching your car in a parking lot or being burdened with high insurance premiums. If you have minimal furniture in your average-sized house, you don't have to worry about cleaning so often. If you have a smaller home in an average neighborhood, you don't have to worry about paying high monthly mortgage and property tax payments. Keep life simple by having fewer things; less is more.

The key to having a good life is to keep everything simple. Don't keep dramatic people around you, have a straightforward type of business, keep communication succinct and simple, and do routine things that make you happy. It's that simple!

Keep life simple by having fewer things; less is more.

The trick to having more daily appreciation is to make it a treat. You will appreciate it more if it's not always available. You don't want to get numb to it. Scarcity is good, and abundance is the enemy of appreciation. Knowing that you can't have access to it all the time makes you appreciate it more. For example, instead of taking trips all the time, I should only go on trips as a reward when I celebrate success.

I find more pleasure when spending money on others than on myself. I like buying gifts for others, or better yet, buying gift certificates for them, so they can take me out to coffee when they use it for the first time. It's pro-social and charitable all at the same time.

Before spending any money, ask yourself if it is happy money or just adds more complexity and drama to your life. Then the choice is easy.

When you have an experience you can share with others, it brings you closer to other people. It will be a story you will enjoy retelling and will give others a sense of who you are. It doesn't matter if it's a long or short story; it will make a long-lasting impression.

As I matured, I started a pruning process; I trim away people or things that don't give me joy. For example, it's normal to have fewer friends as you age because you have become more intelligent and only want to hang out with people who make you happy.

Before spending any money, ask yourself if it is happy money or just adds more complexity and drama to your life.

I never sacrifice my time for money. If you don't like doing chores around the house, hire someone else to do it for you. If you need to change the oil in your car, take it to a shop. And when you are traveling, instead of getting the cheapest flight (probably a red-eye flight), pay more so you can arrive at whatever time you choose. If you can afford it, spend a little money so you can be happier.

Splurge on activities that guarantee a good mood, such as exercise, mediation, reading, family & friends, and sex.

Whenever you can buy time with money, do it. Remember, time is something you can never get back, and you can always make more money if you are healthy. When making a decision, always focus on time instead of money; that way, you will make better and happier choices.

I recently leased a Tesla after years of thinking about it. I have never paid more than 20 thousand dollars for a car, and I have never purchased a new car in my life. That's why it took me three years to pull the trigger on a fifty thousand dollar vehicle. It turned out to be the best decision I ever made.

The autopilot feature is a godsend since I never liked driving long distances. Tesla turns a painful driving experience into something fun and productive. Best money I ever spent! Because of this, I am not wasting money on material things; instead, I am buying an exceptional driving experience with an electric vehicle. The takeaway here is to splurge on experiences that make you happy!

Somehow, life always has a way of becoming complicated. Do whatever you can to keep it simple; you will never regret it.

Chapter 40: Retirement & Charity

Studies have shown that if you retire at 63, you will be dead by 65! The reason is that the human body is not built to be work until such an old age. Unfortunately, our bodies break down with age, so the earlier you can retire, the better. When I talk about retirement, I do not mean that you just sit around and do nothing every day. On the contrary, it's the perfect time to pursue your newfound hobbies or take on rewarding, part-time work to keep your days busy. Everyone needs to have a reason to wake up in the morning and live life with a purpose. A good friend of mine, Bill, suggests that everyone should try to achieve financial freedom by using the first halves of their lives working and the second having fun with their money. Not a bad idea! That's the goal everyone should strive for.

How do you know if you are spending your time wisely? It's easy. If you don't have any time left in your life and still choose to do the same things you are doing now, you are on the right track to living your best life. Think about that for a second. If someone tells you that the world is coming to an end tomorrow, and you still choose to do the same things, that means you have lived a fulfilled and joyful life and don't have any regrets. You have done everything that you wanted to do! Isn't that the best way to leave this world? When you are doing your same routine until your very last moment on earth, that's true happiness.

I do a lot of charity work. I often volunteer with the local homeless shelter or St. Mary church. I prefer volunteering with physical labor to donating money. This way, I know I am actually "doing something" to serve others instead of giving money to a cause where it doesn't necessarily reach the people who need it most. On the topic of philanthropy, I have a different take than most people. I think the reason I donate my precious time is not that I am the most charitable guy in the world; it's because doing so gives me the happiness of knowing that I am helping someone in this world live a better life. I am actually volunteering for a selfish reason. I do it to make myself feel good! I also know that the more I give, the more I will receive. That's a win-win situation, and there's nothing wrong with that.

Every month, I try to donate 5-10% of my monthly income to charity. I contribute to PETA, the American Heart Association, and the American Cancer Society. I have a close association with those charities since I am an animal lover and have lost love ones to cancer and heart disease. I encourage you to give away some money every month; nothing makes a person happier than helping others. Charitable people also tend to live longer and happier lives.

If you genuinely enjoy what you do, then why retire? Maybe you can just scale back on how much time you spend at work, or better yet, if you own your own company, you can dictate what hours you want to work, if any. The desire to do something can keep one alive for a very long time. That's why you must always have a goal, no matter how old you are.

I know many people consider buying a second vacation home in their retirement. My advice, don't do it! It's just a money pit. A while back, I thought about splurging on a vacation home. Since I am a numbers guy, I calculated all the expenses and listed the pros and cons of owning a second home. My conclusion is that paying for an Airbnb is a way better option than owning a second home. The cost of owning a second home is just outrageous, not to mention the money and time cost of maintaining it when you are away. It's just not worth it, no matter how much money one has.

We live on borrowed time, so there is no need to be afraid of death. Fear of death does not prevent death; it prevents life. On the other side of fear is freedom, so deal with it head-on. Instead of being scared of dying, find enjoyment and fulfillment in the smallest things in nature - forests, beaches, green fields, farms, lakes, and mountains. Life is so short, so we might as well enjoy it while it lasts. For me personally, I travel as much as I can. I am a collector of incredible experiences, not a consumer of material things. When facing life's end, strive for no attachments and no regrets. Let your goal be to depart this world thinking that this has been a very fulfilled life and hoping that you have helped and served others.

My mentality is to live world-class twenty-four hours a day, seven days a week. This means eating the most delicious food at Michelin-rated restaurants, having coffee at 7-star hotels, sitting courtside at NBA games, and listening to joyful classical music in Paris. Splurge a little. You are retired!

Chapter 41: Becoming a Monetized YouTuber in 3 weeks

As I am finishing up writing this book in late June 2021, we are in the middle of the baseball season, where Japanese 2-way baseball player Shohei Ohtani is tearing up the Major League. He is currently hitting over 30 home runs and is also a dominating pitcher on the mount. For those of you that don't watch baseball, it is very difficult to be a hitter and also a pitcher at the same time. The last person that did it was the famous Babe Ruth over 100 years ago. Anyhow, I am also a big fan of Shohei Ohtani. So I went to one of his baseball games at the end of June, where he was pitching and hitting. I was at the game early and watched Ohtani warming up in the bullpen before the game. I took several close-up videos of him stretching and throwing some warm-up tosses. I used my new iPhone, and the resolution was excellent. The videos I took were pretty good, and they all look like a professional videographer took them.

I had lots of fun at the game as I watched him play. When I get home that night, I posted some of the videos on my social media page. A couple of days later, some of my friends on Facebook told me that those videos were perfect and that I should post them on YouTube. So I did. I created a channel called "Jason's Japanese MLB" and posted all my videos from that day to the channel. To my surprise, I got tons of views on the videos I posted! Most of the audience was from Japan. Likely due to the Pandemic, very few Japanese reporters were following Ohtani around the country as traveling was still restricted due to the Covid-19 Delta variant. So fans in Japan were relying on global TV stations such ESPN or MLB Online for news on Ohtani, where they only offered limited coverage.

I sensed an opportunity here. Since Ohtani was doing so well on the field and on the mount, there was a big following in the world, especially from fans in Japan. So I decided to take a trip to Los Angeles Angels Stadium the following weekend to get some more videos of Ohtani to post on YouTube. Since the Angels Stadium is about a 6-hour drive from my house, I had lots of time to think about how to make my videos appeal to Japanese fans. I came up with some video topics that might be of interest:

1) Videos of Ohtani interacting with his teammates and his fans
2) Videos of fans cheering for him
3) Videos of Ohtani in action, pitching and hitting home runs
4) Video of the fans buying Ohtani gear at the souvenir store
5) Videos of fans getting free Ohtani pillows (there was a promotion where Angels gave away free pillows with Ohtani pictures on them to the first 15,000 fans)
6) Video of me interviewing fans talking about Ohtani

As you can see, my goal was to make Ohtani-related videos that fans in Japan wouldn't be able to see on ESPN. More "personal" stories of Ohtani would be my "niche." Long story short, I attended a game on Monday and another game on Tuesday. I took about 30-40 videos from those two days.

Now it was time for me to post them online. But to do that, I had to teach myself how to do simple video editing so my videos would run smoothly together. I went online and spent about 3 hours viewing videos about how to edit videos using an iPhone app called iMovie. I also had to be creative in my video headlines to attract attention. So instead of using the headline, "Ohtani throwing warm-up toss before the game," I would write, "Ohtani throwing over 100 miles an hour fastballs even in the warm-up!". I also learned that few Japanese people speak or read English, so I needed to translate text to Japanese to attract those fans. After about three straight days of working 12 hours a day, I finally posted all the videos online. Now I just needed to wait and see if I could actually get people to watch my new videos. In the meantime, I spent another 6 hours researching how to become a

Millionaire Success Secrets

"YouTuber," where a person is compensated or monetized for their YouTube videos. The requirement is to have 1000 subscribers and over 4000 public watchable hours. I had no idea what that terminology meant, so I had to do some research.

I watched videos of reputable YouTubers explaining how to reach those goals. They suggested niche videos and various ways of marketing those videos to specific audiences. I learned so much by watching their videos. Most YouTubers said it took them about two years to meet those two requirements, and it's essential to have at least one video posted every week. They also said that being a full-time YouTuber was hard work. They work about 50 hours per week between making videos and editing, so it is not easy. It is fascinating for me to learn about becoming a Youtuber. The only thing I don't like is working long hours, but I still decided to continue doing this YouTube thing because I enjoy watching Ohtani playing baseball. Thus, money is not and should not be the sole motivation to do this.

While researching YouTube videos, I also realized I had made several mistakes. There are two types of videos; one is just a regular video, another one is called a "YouTube short," where the video is taken vertically and needs to be less than 1 minute long. I guess that's YouTube's strategy to compete with another app called TikTok! However, YouTube Shorts videos are NOT counted as public watch hours and are also not monetized. Also, any videos with copyright music in the background will not be monetized. That hurt me since I specifically took a lot of short videos thinking it would be a good way to market my channel and accumulate watchable hours. In addition, baseball stadiums play music while the game is on, so almost all my videos have some copyrighted music in there. What I could have done was to have non-copyright music replace the existing copyrighted music. Anyways, the result was that I lost many public watchable hours, and it will take me longer to meet the qualification of 1000 subscribers and 4000 watchable hours. Instead of getting frustrated and down on myself, I just worked a little harder. I went through all the videos I had of Ohtani and found many little clips of the video which potential viewers might find interesting. So instead of having one long video, I had multiple shorter videos that are interesting and will generate more viewership.

I also had to learn how to market my videos. I realized I had to create YouTube thumbnails to attract potential viewers choosing my videos over other recommended videos. I also looked through all the comments from my viewers to see what they liked or disliked. I found that Japanese people mainly want to see Ohtani in a positive light, so videos of Ohtani being respectful to the elderly and getting along with his teammates received many "likes." Thus, I should post more videos like this and cater to those viewers by having headlines such as "Ohtani is a very well-mannered young man." Those headlines get more clicks than others. In addition, I would also include some controversial headlines that would get emotional reactions, such as "Why is Ohtani taking his hat off when the US national anthem is playing?" Again, those types of headlines get me tons of clicks.

Some of the viewers' comments suggested that the headlines I used were not "proper Japanese." I guess google translator does a poor job of translating. A lot of the headlines I use do not reflect what I mean to say. But viewers can kind of still understand the point I am trying to get across. I was going to hire a native Japanese speaker to help me make my headlines better, but I decided against it. Having poor Japanese headlines might just be my niche! Looking at the "poorly worded Japanese headline," the viewers know I am not a native Japanese speaker, so my view of Ohtani is from an American's perspective. So no matter how crazy or insane my video headlines sound, they are more acceptable to them since I am a foreigner. I leveraged my weakness into my strength!

I went to the games on July 5 and July 6, and I worked over 12 hours a day to finish posting all my videos by July 8. After I finished all the postings, my eyeballs were bulging because I looked at my computer screen so much! So I decided to take a couple of days off from working on YouTube. The next time I went on YouTube again was on July 10th. Remember I mentioned that most people take two years to meet the YouTube monetization requirements of having 1000 subscribers and 4000 watchable hours? I did it! I not only met and surpassed the requirements, I probably shattered the record of how fast a person can meet the YouTube monetization requirements. See below.

ADVANCED MODE

Jun 26 – Jul 10, 2021
Custom

Realtime
● Updating live

3,628
Subscribers

SEE LIVE COUNT

1,624,027
Views · Last 48 hours

In a little over two weeks, I had 3628 subscribers and 12,032+ public watch hours! I was so excited. I applied for monetization right away. And on July 12, 2021, I was approved! So now I am officially a monetized YouTuber!

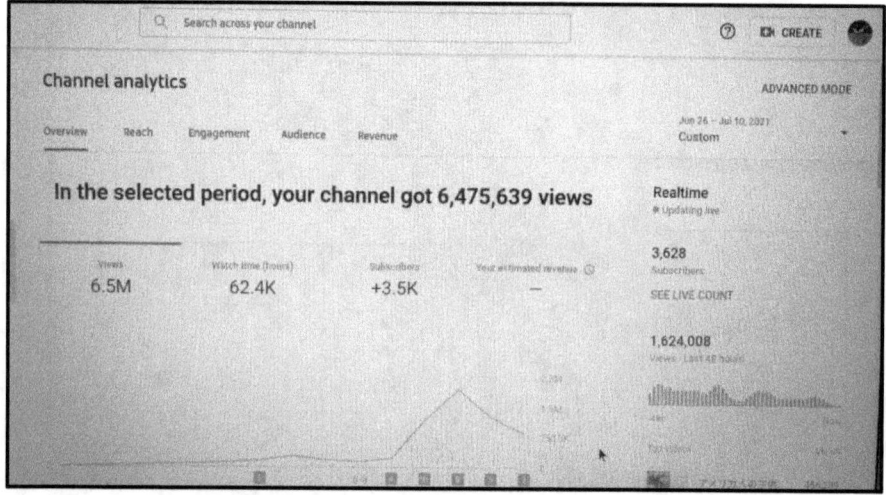

The moral of the story is as follows:

1) Do something you have passion for, and then it doesn't feel like work anymore. For example, I am a big baseball fan, and I love watching Shohei Otani play, so videotaping him does not feel like work to me.

2) Take the time to strategize and make a business plan. It makes execution much more efficient and productive.

3) Be very observant of opportunities around you. For example, when I went to the first Ohtani game, I was just there to enjoy a ball game. I never thought of becoming a YouTuber. It just came to me. It's similar to the saying, "when an opportunity comes knocking, you better be ready."

4) Never listen to naysayers. I did not give up on becoming a monetized YouTuber after listening to others saying it will take at least two years to meet the requirements. Instead, I spent time thinking about what I

could do to expedite the process. So instead of 2 years, I met the goal in 2 weeks. If I can do it, anyone can!

Chapter 42: Conclusion

So we here at the end of my book. I have shared much of what I have learned in my life and career. I was lucky to be able to get back up after many obstacles and challenges. Trust me, there are plenty of them! Fortunately, I always learned something from those difficult times. I hope that by sharing those experiences with you, you can avoid some of the mistakes I made and be well on your way to success.

I love the saying, "Learning without execution is useless," so take what you have learned from this book and go out and build wealth and grow passive income. Right now, I want you to grab a piece of paper and write down all the "action steps" you can do now to get yourself moving in the right direction. They could include starting a morning ritual, reading more books, or something as simple as being grateful and saying thank you three times as soon as you wake up. No matter how small of a step you take, make a change in the right direction to better yourself. The fact that you picked up this book tells me that you have every intention of taking steps to better your life. I hope I have helped you by giving you some pointers on what you can do now. If I only helped one person make a change to better their lives, I have achieved my purpose in writing this book. All the effort was well worth it. Good luck everyone, I am rooting for you!

Thank you. Thank you. Thank you! I hope you have enjoyed this book. As this is only my second book, it would mean a lot to me if you could post a review on Amazon to let me know how I did. Thank you in advance for giving me comments and suggestions so I can continue to grow and improve.

Chapter 43: Book Recommendations

1) Don't sweat the small stuff and it's all small stuff by Richard Carlson
2) The Happiness Track by Ema Seppala
3) Success Affirmations by Jack Canfield
4) The happiness advantage by Shawn Achor
5) The slight edge by Jeff Olson
6) Happy money by Ken Honda
7) The power of intention by Wayne Dyer
8) Little things matter by W. Todd Smith
9) Success thought a positive mental attitude by Napoleon Hill
10) What to say when you talk to yourself by Shad Helmstetter
11) The 1% rule by Tommy Baker
12) How to build self-discipline by Martin Meadows

www.ingramcontent.com/pod-product-compliance
Lightning Source LLC
Chambersburg PA
CBHW072029230526
45466CB00020B/1182